Chambers
language builder

'This book does what it says: it systematically and creatively builds understanding of how language works. The range of activities, the accurate analysis throughout and the intelligent use of a corpus of real English are all excellent, while the chapters on 'word families' and 'linking sentences to make texts' are simply outstanding. The book is right in tune with National Curriculum requirements, the presentation is spot on and both students and teachers cannot fail to benefit from the high quality in evidence from beginning to end.'

Ronald Carter, Professor of Modern English Language, University of Nottingham; also consultant and developer, Qualifications and Curriculum Authority.

'This superb book takes an eminently sensible approach to the complexities of English grammar. It covers everything the student needs to know about word class, sentence structure and word families, and it goes beyond these topics to talk about grammar choices, effective writing style, and about English as a constantly changing language. The book is written with authority and depth of knowledge, yet with a lightness of touch that makes it accessible and relevant to everyday English.'

Professor Susan Hunston, Head of Department of English, University of Birmingham.

Chambers

CHAMBERS
An imprint of Chambers Harrap Publishers Ltd
7 Hopetoun Crescent
Edinburgh, EH7 4AY

First published by Chambers Harrap Publishers Ltd 2008

A CIP catalogue record for this book is available from the British Library.

ISBN 978 0550 10340 6

Extract from speech by Winston Churchill reproduced with permission of
Curtis Brown Ltd, London on behalf of The Estate of Winston Churchill ©
Winston Churchill; extract from The Twits © Roald Dahl (published by
Jonathan Cape and Penguin Books Ltd) reproduced by permission of
David Higham Associates.

Designed and typeset by Chambers Harrap Publishers Ltd, Edinburgh
Printed in Italy by Legoprint

Contents

Contributors

Editor
Mary O'Neill

Illustrations
Richard Duszczak

Teacher Consultants
Jane Cooper
Rachel Rowling

Prepress Controller
Andrew Butterworth

Corpus Developer
Ruth O'Donovan

Acknowledgements

I would like first and foremost to thank Andrew Dickinson, for his unfailing help and support. I would also like to acknowledge my debt to John Sinclair (1933–2007), who did so much to pioneer and promote the use of large natural-language corpora in language learning and grammatical description. Thanks also to my patient and efficient editor, Mary O'Neill, to Ruth O'Donovan, who does clever things with corpora, to the teachers who have commented on the text, and finally to Maisie, my 13-year-old 'consultant'.

Gill Francis

Introduction

A firm grasp of the English language is vital for communication, and a knowledge of grammatical concepts and terms is an essential foundation on which to build language skills. *Chambers Language Builder* not only gives students the tools and terminology they need to convey their critical understanding of texts and how they are crafted, but also encourages both creativity and accuracy in the choice of grammatical forms and constructions.

However, it is far from a traditional, stuffy school grammar, full of rules and their many exceptions. Every effort has been made to ensure the text will appeal to its audience and is relevant to their needs. It does not attempt to cover English in all its complexity but clearly explains the key ideas that young students really need in order to understand how language works, from word classes to clause and sentence types, as well as how sentences can be combined to form coherent and interesting texts.

Whenever a new idea is presented, numerous examples illustrate and reinforce the idea. Unlike other school texts, these examples are 'real-world' examples taken from Chambers' unique and extensive corpus of written and spoken language. As a result, the examples sound natural and interesting and, what's more, they are a *true* reflection of the structures of English in use. Very often, a short activity will follow the examples so that students can test themselves and make sure that they understand the idea correctly. The answers can be checked on pages 181 to 211 at the back of the book.

To give the text further appeal, additional boxes provide tips on, for example, skilled use of language features, standard and non-standard usage, language change, and punctuation. Humorous illustrations lift the page but also consolidate the terminology by acting as a visual aid to memory.

Chambers Language Builder has been written and designed with the expert advice of teachers of English, and complements the Key Stage 3/4 programmes of study in England and Wales, the Key Stage 3/4 Curriculum in Northern Ireland and the National Guidelines in Scotland. It is an indispensable handbook for the secondary curriculum.

This book contains lots of additional pieces of information, marked out in blue.

 This highlights information on standard and non-standard English, and how you can use language correctly.

 This marks information about punctuation and how you can use it properly.

 This introduces tips on how you can use English more effectively.

Word class:
the four main classes

Part 1

What is word class?

There are two things to think about when you try to put words into classes. The first is the different kinds of **work that words do** in a sentence. The second is **the way words behave** – how they combine with other words to make meanings. Words that behave in the same way tend to belong to the same class.

The work that words do

Look at these sentences, especially the words in italic.

1 Let's take a fresh look at the *finances*.
2 I don't know the first thing about the *economy*.
3 We're facing a serious *economic* crisis.
4 Milan is Italy's *financial* capital.

The words in bold italic in 1 and 2 are both **nouns**, and in 3 and 4 they are both **adjectives**. You can't swap around the nouns and adjectives, as the sentences wouldn't make sense.

   ✗ Let's take a fresh look at the financial.
   ✗ Milan is Italy's finances capital.

This is because nouns and adjectives do different work. The nouns in 1 and 2 are answering the question 'what?' and the adjectives in 3 and 4 are answering the question 'what kind?'. These are just two examples of the type of job that words do.

❖ **Activity 1 Before you start**

Look at these sentences and decide which of the words in **bold** can be exchanged with each other.

1 This is more complicated than I **imagined**.

2 It is an extremely **imaginative** and interesting novel, definitely one of her best.

3 I was impressed by Maisie's honesty, **thoughtfulness**, and insight.

What is word class?

4 For one terrible second he **thought** that another body had been found.

5 No-one who met Jerzi could forget his sense of humour, his **imagination**, or his courage.

6 This is a very **thoughtful** and original piece of work.

The words in bold belong to three different word classes. Can you guess which these are?

 Identifying different word classes

A lot of words belong to more than one class, for example *sleep* is both a verb and a noun, and *light* is both an adjective and a noun.

   *It gets **light** early in the summer.* (adjective)

   *There was not enough **light** to see where we were going.* (noun)

In any sentence, you will usually be able to tell which it is, because of the work it is doing and the words it occurs with.

There are eight main word classes, all with different roles to play in sentences:

- nouns
- verbs
- adjectives
- adverbs
- pronouns
- determiners
- prepositions
- conjunctions

Part 1 will concentrate on the first four of these: nouns, verbs, adjectives and adverbs. These are **open classes**. This means that there are thousands and thousands of words in each class, and new ones are coming into the language all the time (more recent examples include *globalization*, *downsizing*, *podcast*, *download*, and *proactive*, to mention just a few).

Part 2 will deal with the second four word classes: pronouns, determiners, prepositions and conjunctions. These are all **closed classes** – this means that there is a fixed number of words in each, and with a few exceptions, no new ones come into the language.

The way words behave

The second way to decide on a word's class is to look at its surroundings. Words of different classes combine with other words in different ways. For example, **determiners** (like *a* and *the*) often come before **nouns**, and so do **adjectives** (like *enormous, little, shiny* and *bald*).

> ⊳ He was *a* man of *enormous* size, with *a little shiny bald* head.

Adverbs often come before **adjectives**.

> ⊳ We both found the film *incredibly* funny.

Look back at two of the sentences from page 3.

> ⊳ I don't know the first thing about *the economy*.
> ⊳ We're facing a serious *economic* crisis.

You know that *economy* is a noun because it has *the* in front of it. You know that *economic* is an adjective because it comes before the noun *crisis*.

The next sections will say a little more about the ways in which you link words together to make meanings, but this will be explained more fully in Part 4.

Nouns

The work that nouns do: concrete, abstract and proper nouns

You often hear nouns defined as 'naming' words – they **identify** a person, thing, situation or idea. There are three kinds of noun:

Concrete nouns refer to people and objects that you can see, hear or touch, like *ship*, *cat*, *car*, *computer* and *wood*.

Abstract nouns refer to ideas, qualities and situations, like *problem*, *strength*, *hope*, *despair* and *meaning*.

> The **beach** is part of my **life**. I love the **idea** of wearing a **sarong**, with **hair** down to my **waist** and my **kids** playing in the **sand.**

In the example above, *beach*, *sarong*, *hair*, *waist*, *kids* and *sand* are concrete. *Part*, *life* and *idea* are abstract.

The distinction is not always easy to see. For example, *camouflage* is something visible (if you can see it at all!) but it is also a concept, an ability that some animals have, for example.

❖ **Activity 2 Concrete and abstract nouns**
Decide whether the nouns in **bold** are abstract or concrete. Which are difficult to classify, and why do you think this is?

1 A small glass **lamp** bloomed with a tiny **flame** to light the darkening **space**. Now, like an **onion** peeling, the outermost **layer** of the **pod**'s **walls** had begun to fold back. Translucent walls transformed to fine **crystal**, opening a clear **view** to the **seas** beyond the pod.

2 All the things **science** had promised us hadn't come to pass. **Disease** was still a **problem**. **Starvation** was still a problem. **Violence** and **crime** and **war** were still problems.

3 Then she heard the **panther**'s **growl** again. The black **shape** slid into **sight** just a few **yards** away. She remembered the **intelligence** in its **eyes**.

In your writing, try to use a variety of concrete and abstract nouns. A text containing mainly concrete nouns tends to seem unimaginative. As soon as you start giving your own thoughts and opinions, you will need to use lots of abstract nouns.

Proper nouns name people, countries, continents, geographical areas like mountain ranges and oceans, organizations, restaurants, companies and so on. You can spot these easily, as they begin with capital letters. Some of them include the word *the*.

the United Nations	*Queen Victoria*	*Venezuela*
Phillip Pullman	*the Himalayas*	*The Sun*
The Da Vinci Code	*the London Eye*	*Europe*

Nouns

❖ **Activity 3 Proper nouns**
Match the two halves of these proper nouns. Add 'the' if necessary.

1	Labour	**a**	Parliament
2	Taj	**b**	Kilimanjaro
3	South	**c**	Party
4	Mount	**d**	Mahal
5	European	**e**	Africa

You can use any of these types of noun on its own to identify something, but you usually need to combine it with other words, so that it can identify more complicated things. Together the noun and the other words make a noun group. These are just two examples of noun groups.

adjective + **noun**	*fresh* **fruit**	*natural* **energy**
determiner + noun + **noun**	*a fitness* **class**	*a football* **hero**

Note here that nouns are used before other nouns, just like adjectives.

It is usually noun groups, rather than single nouns, that do the work of identifying people and things and giving them particular descriptions.

See Part 4, page 111 for more information about noun groups.

Noun forms

A noun usually changes its form when it is **plural**. Most nouns add -s or -es, like *boy* ➔ *boys* or *fox* ➔ *foxes*. Nouns that end in a **consonant** + -y change the -y to -ies, as in *country* ➔ *countries*. But there are some **irregular** plurals like *child* ➔ *children* and *wife* ➔ *wives*.

❖ **Activity 4 Irregular plural nouns**
Write down the plurals of these words.

leaf   foot   mouse   woman   crisis   valley   half   fish   sheep

There is one word that can have two different plurals. Which is it?

8

Many nouns, such as *fishing*, *teaching*, *meeting* and *building* end in *-ing*. The *-ing* form is also one form of the verb (see page 18), so you may find this confusing. But you can usually tell whether an *-ing* word is a noun or a verb because of the work it is doing in the sentence.

> ▸ **Teaching** is a lot like lion-taming. (noun)
> ▸ Hospital staff are **teaching** her how to walk again. (verb)

❖ **Activity 5 Identifying nouns**
Which of the '-ing' forms in these sentences are nouns and which are verbs? How can you tell?

1 They haven't been given adequate training.

2 I hated the name from the very beginning.

3 They were all beginning school at the same time.

4 Alpine resorts are suffering from a lack of snow this season.

5 I'll probably be training on Monday again.

6 Lucy seemed to be blind to their suffering.

All the **colours** are also nouns (though they are adjectives as well – see page 32).

> ▸ Jon's face had gone a deathly **white.**

Types of noun
By 'types of noun' of noun here, we are talking about nouns that behave differently in grammatical ways. The main types are **count nouns** (sometimes called **countable** nouns) and **uncount nouns** (sometimes called **uncountable** nouns).

Count nouns
Count nouns are nouns that have both **singular** and **plural** forms. They refer to people and things that can be counted – you can have one or more than one of them. To make the plural, you usually add *-s* or *-es*.

When a count noun is followed by a verb, you have to be sure that the verb 'agrees' with it.

> ▸ That **seagull** *is driving* me crazy.
> ▸ Those **seagulls** *are driving* me crazy.
> ✗ Those seagulls is driving me crazy.

The most common count nouns in English are *year*, *way*, *day*, *thing*, *time*, *man* and *part*.

When a count noun is **singular**, it must have some sort of **determiner** before it (see Part 2, page 63). The most common determiners are *the*, *a*, *this*, *his* and *her*. When a count noun is **plural**, it can be used alone.

> ▸ I had *a* **cat** that only went out at night.
> ✗ I had cat that only went out at night.
> ▸ **Cats** don't always eat their prey.

Uncount nouns

Uncount nouns have only one form – they have no plural. Uncount nouns usually refer to abstract things like *advice*, *luck*, *poverty* and *progress*, or else to substances like *blood*, *electricity*, *milk*, *sugar* and *smoke*.

> **Did you know…?** Funnily enough, *money* is an uncount noun. It may be the most counted thing in the world, but you can't say ✗ *one money, two moneys*.

You can use uncount nouns with or without a determiner. You don't usually use *a*.

> ▸ Islanders feared that **pollution** from the mine would damage water supplies.
> ▸ Ecologists view with dismay *the* **pollution** of our air, rivers and seas.

❖ **Activity 6 Count and uncount nouns (1)**
Discuss whether the nouns in **bold** are count or uncount.

1 When you breathe in, oxygenated **air** inflates your **lungs**. **Blood** circulating in the lungs exchanges **carbon dioxide** for the **oxygen** in the air.

2 Jamie has no **money** and no **job**, and is getting very little **support** from his **friends**. He has few **opportunities**, and not much **hope** of a good **career**.

When you want to give an exact quantity of an uncount noun, you use structures like *a piece of **advice***, *two litres of **blood*** and *three spoonfuls of **sugar***.

Nouns that are both count and uncount

A huge number of nouns behave in a way that is typical of **both** count and uncount nouns. For example, the most common noun in English, *time*, is a perfectly ordinary count noun in these examples:

▸ Choose *a **time*** when you are reasonably relaxed.
▸ There are ***times*** when you simply have to take a stand.

But *time*, with a slightly different meaning, is also uncount, as these sayings show:

Time flies.   **Time** *is a great healer.*   **Time** *is money.*

❖ **Activity 7 Count and uncount nouns (2)**
In which sentences is the noun 'crime' count, and in which is it uncount?

1 Forgery and fraud are both serious crimes.

2 Petty crime always seems to increase at Christmas.

3 DNA evidence proved that he had not committed the crime.

4 Remember the slogan 'Tough on crime and tough on the causes of crime'?

5 Mary has never actually been charged with a crime.

Nouns

Collective nouns

A few nouns, such as *team, committee, government* and *audience* are **collective** nouns. Collective nouns refer to a group of people or things. When they are singular they can be followed by either a singular or a plural verb, according to whether you are thinking of the group as a unit, or as individuals.

> The **team** *is* better prepared this time.
> The **team** *are* under unbearable pressure – every one of them.

Verbs

The work that verbs do

A verb tells you what is happening in a sentence, or what people are doing. This is why it is often defined as a 'doing' word.

> I **showered** and **dressed**, then Keiko **met** me with a cup of coffee and **told** me the phone **had been ringing** all morning.

But not all verbs are about actions. Some of the most common verbs in English are *be*, *have*, *know*, *see* and *want*.

> He and I **were** friends, that's all.
> You **think** I **know** anything about it?

Verbs

❖ **Activity 8 Before you start**
Can you guess which verbs are missing from these sentences? Think of more than one verb wherever possible.

1 I _____ home and _____ some more football, _____ channels whenever they _____ a commercial.

2 Winston _____ his eyebrows and _____ at me in surprise.

3 Andy _____ me to _____ him your number, but I _____.

4 We dashed across the car park, _____ our cases into the car, and _____ off.

5 I _____ my left ankle while _____ football.

6 Farmers now _____ it harder and harder to _____ a living.

So verbs also tell you about what things are and what someone's mental 'landscape' is like – what they know and think and feel.

You also use verbs to describe situations – what things look like or how things are arranged, for example.

▸ The upper floors *were divided* into single rooms that lined a long, bright hallway. Women *were housed* on the second floor, men on the third.

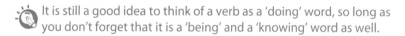 It is still a good idea to think of a verb as a 'doing' word, so long as you don't forget that it is a 'being' and a 'knowing' word as well.

Verb forms

We saw on page 8 that nouns change their forms to make plurals, but verbs have more different forms than nouns. For example, you can say:

*I **remember**, she **remembers**, we **remembered**, and I was **remembering**.*

❖ **Activity 9 Verb forms**

Which form of 'remember' would you put in the gaps? Is there more than one possibility?

1 He suddenly _____ a boy at school who'd looked exactly the same as Matt.

2 The police want her to revisit the scene in the hope that she may _____ a vital clue.

3 _____ , this is a long trip and you'll need to be prepared for the jetlag.

4 I wanted to _____ every moment of that day for ever.

5 You could at least have _____ to water the plants!

Irregular verbs

The verb *remember* is 'regular': to make its different forms you add *-s*, *-ed*, and *-ing*. But there are over a hundred common 'irregular' verbs that change in other ways, and you have to learn to spell them all! *Break, eat, buy, bring* and *know* are some examples. Using *break*, you can say:

I **break** *it, it* **breaks** *easily, it* **broke**, *you've* **broken** *it, and my heart is* **breaking**.

❖ **Activity 10 Irregular verbs**

Try to make a list of ten other verbs that are different from 'remember' in that you do not make their different tenses by adding '-ed'. Write down their forms.

To start you off:

go, went, gone

buy, bought, bought

...

The way all these forms are used is explained in the next few pages.

Verbs

Auxiliaries

Auxiliaries are small verbs that are used with different verb forms (**main verbs**) like *remember* and *break* in order to build **verb chains**. There are three auxiliary verbs, all of which have different forms:

- *do*, *does*, *did*
- *be*, *am*, *is*, *are*, *was*, *were*, *been*
- *have*, *has*, *had*

❖ **Activity 11 Before you start**
Which auxiliaries would fit with these verb forms? Is there more than one possibility?

1 Where _____ you **buy** that?

2 The British _____ **eaten** eels for centuries.

3 When she reached them, she _____ **smiling** broadly.

4 I thought you _____ **left** ages ago!

5 Guide dogs _____ **allowed**, but the Peke stays outside.

You will now see how verb chains are formed and what different sorts of chains mean and do.

Tense

Some verb chains tell you the **time** of an event or situation – in the past, the present or the future. The word **tense** refers to the way the verb changes to express this meaning. You form different tenses using different auxiliaries and verb forms.

The present and past tenses

To make the **present** tense, you use the simplest form of the verb, like *remember* or *break*. This is often called the **infinitive** (see page 29).

You put an -s on the end when the **subject** (the 'doer' of an action) is *he* or *she* or a name, for example.

▸ She usually ***gets*** most of the answers right.

> *Tom **likes** sparkling water.*

You use the auxiliaries **do** and **does** with an infinitive to ask questions in the present tense.

>) **Do** you always **tell** the truth?
>) How **does** your camera **work**?

You also use **do** and **does** with *not* to make the **negative** in the present.

>) I go to the gym, but I **don't like** it much.

❖ **Activity 12 Auxiliaries – present tense**
   Fill in the gaps using **do, don't, does** or **doesn't**.

1 At the moment I _____ see what any of this means.

2 Why _____ you wear your red dress with the silver belt?

3 Even if they are wrong, what difference _____ it make?

4 I think Maria's family _____ like the English weather at all.

5 '_____ spiders ever get tired of climbing walls?' she
   wondered.

Is there more than one possibility for any of these? What kind of
noun is 'family'? (See page 12.)

To make the **past** tense, you add **-ed** to the infinitive if the verb is regular.
Irregular verbs have different past tenses:

go → went   *see → saw*   *eat → ate*

You use the auxiliary **did** with an infinitive to ask questions in the past tense,
and with *not* for the negative.

>) In which role **did** she **become** famous?
>) I entered the restaurant, hoping I **didn't look** too dangerous or
>   insane.

These three auxiliaries – *do, does* and *did* – are sometimes used to give
emphasis.

>) I'm not planning to drop out as I **do want** a degree.

Verbs

In speech and in most writing (though not in very formal writing), you often use the negative **contractions** *don't*, *doesn't* and *didn't*. The word 'contraction' just means that one or more letters have been left out and the words have been joined.

 Remember that with *do*, *does* and *did* you always use the **infinitive** of the verb – the simplest form with no endings.

✓ *Did he **leave**?*

✗ *Did he left?*

❖ **Activity 13 Auxiliaries – present and past tense**
Put **do**, **does** or **did** into the sentences. Is there more than one possibility?

1 I like Leroy because he _____**n't disrespect** my beliefs.

2 _____ she **give** you any clue as to her real identity?

3 What on earth _____ they **talk** about all day?

4 Call me if his condition worsens, but I _____**n't think** it will.

5 I _____**n't eat** much junk food, but I _____ **like** an occasional bag of crisps.

Say whether each sentence is in the present or past tense.

Present and past continuous

You add *-ing* to the infinitive of the verb and use it with the different forms of the auxiliary **be** (*am*, *is*, *are*) to make another present tense. This is often used to talk about ongoing actions or situations, and is usually called the **present continuous**.

▸ I ***am enjoying*** my time here.

▸ The sun ***is shining*** and the birds ***are singing*** in the trees.

You often use the contractions *I'm*, *you're*, *he's*, *it's*, *we're* and *they're*.

 Punctuation: Remember that when you use *it's* to mean *it is*, as in *it's raining*, you must put an apostrophe. *Its* without an apostrophe is a **determiner** (see page 63), as in *The bus skidded out of control when **its** brakes failed*.

Similarly, when you use *you're* to mean *you are*, you must put in the apostrophe.

✓ *If you can't get same-day delivery, **you're** not in Beds 'R Us.*

✗ *If you can't get same-day delivery, your not in Beds 'R Us.*

You use the same *-ing* form to make the **past continuous** tense, which is often used to talk about continuous actions in the past.

▶ '*I **wasn't thinking** about Firaz.*' '*Who **were** you **thinking** about, then?*'

The **negative** contractions are *isn't*, *aren't* and *weren't*.

 Standard and non-standard: Some people use the contraction *ain't* in speech, for example *I ain't coming*. This is not standard English, though it may be used in other dialects. You should not use it in your writing!

Perfect tenses

There are other past tenses that you form by adding *-ed* to the infinitive and using the auxiliaries **have**, **has** and **had**. These are often called **perfect** tenses.

You use *have* and *has* when you are talking about what happened recently, or how long something has lasted.

> ‣ I **have** just **started** a new IT course.
> ‣ She **has worked** with children since she was sixteen.

You use *had* with the *-ed* form to show that something happened before a particular point in time.

> ‣ The police *arrived* after everyone else **had disappeared** from the scene.

Note that for regular verbs, the past tense form *I* **remembered** is the same as the *-ed* form in *I* **have remembered**. But with **irregular** verbs, the form you use here is not the same as the one you use for the past tense with *did*. You use the **third** of these forms:

break, broke, **broken**   *go, went,* **gone**   *see, saw,* **seen**

> ‣ All the tickets **had gone** by the time we got through.

 Standard and non-standard: Remember to use the right form of irregular verbs. For example, you should write

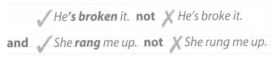

✓ He**'s broken** it. **not** ✗ He's broke it.

and ✓ She **rang** me up. **not** ✗ She rung me up.

You use *have*, *has* and *had* with *been* and the *-ing* form to talk about ongoing actions that started some time ago.

> ‣ He **has been experimenting** with laser surgery for several years.

You often use the contractions *'ve* and *'d*, as in *I've finished*, and the negatives *haven't*, *hasn't* and *hadn't*.

❖ **Activity 14 Auxiliaries – mixed tenses (1)**
Match the two halves of the sentences.

1	More politicians	**a**	has been babysitting the kids.
2	According to health experts, I	**b**	has come up with a solution.
3	My neighbour's daughter	**c**	are hinting at tax increases.
4	Not one person	**d**	have found their ideal home.
5	Paul and Gek Ling	**e**	was simply eating too much.

❖ **Activity 15 Auxiliaries – mixed tenses (2)**
Fill in the gaps using auxiliaries. Use negatives if necessary. There may be more than one possibility.

1 You just _____ know what to believe these days.

2 Mohamed _____ picked up the phone from the desk, and _____ playing with it.

3 This is the worst food I _____ ever tasted.

4 Neither of his books _____ selling very well at the moment.

5 Usually they went for a brisk walk after they _____ eaten.

6 In the 1990s my parents _____ living in Gloucester.

Standard and non-standard: Remember that the subject of a verb has to 'agree with' the verb. You say

✓ We **were** having breakfast. **not** ✗ We was having breakfast.

You say

✓ Large numbers of tourists **visit** London. **not** ✗ Large numbers of tourists visits London.

Future time

It is usually said that there is no **future tense** in English – the verb does not change its form, and you don't use *do, be* or *have* as auxiliaries. When you want to talk about time in the future, you can often use a **present** tense.

▸ My dad*'s running* in the half-marathon tomorrow.
▸ The number 11 bus *leaves* in ten minutes.

Or you can use **modals** like *will* with an infinitive. The negative is *will not* and the contractions are *'ll* and *won't* – not *willn't*, for some strange reason. (For information about other modals, see page 24.)

▸ I*'ll give* him some positive feedback; perhaps it *will encourage* him.
▸ If you feed a starving dog it *won't bite* you.

You can also use *be going to* with an infinitive, especially to talk about what you intend to do, or what you think will happen in the future. To make the negative, add *not* or *n't*.

▸ We*'re going to miss you*.
▸ I just don't know what*'s going to happen* in the future.
▸ I've decided that I*'m not going to make* another album for a while.

Standard and non-standard: When you ask someone a question using *going to*, you write

✓ **Are** you going to...?

You don't write

✗ *You going to...?*

although this is probably the way it sounds when you speak.

❖ **Activity 16 Future time**
Fill in the gaps using an auxiliary so that the sentences refer to future time. Use negatives if necessary.

1 I'm excited about the win, but it _____ change my life.

2 Julie and Wojtek _____ moving to their new house next week.

3 I _____ pay you four pounds an hour if you help with the garden.

4 The electronic version probably _____ going to come online anytime soon.

5 Large amounts of snow _____ probably going to fall over the weekend.

What do the last two sentences tell you about the position of 'probably' in positive and negative sentences?

A note on negatives: You should avoid using 'double negatives' in any tense.

X *I never did nothing!*

✓ *I never did anything!*

X *I'm not going to stand no nonsense!*

✓ *I'm not going to stand any nonsense!*

Consistency of tense

When you are writing, you are in a particular '**time frame**'. It is important to use the tenses that are right for this time frame (past, present or future).

All the verbs in this extract are in the same time frame:

> He **led** me into a kitchen and **sat** me down at a table where I **drank** some tea while he prepared breakfast. He **was telling** me enthusiastically about his cooking skills, but he **burnt** the bacon and **overcooked** the eggs.

Both the tenses used are **past**. In the next example, the tense changes.

> The previous night, Fumio **had promised** to give me a lift to the ferry terminal. While he **made** his morning calls, I **visited** the tourist office and **looked** at the timetable.

There are two time frames here, the previous night and the morning. The **perfect** tense formed with *had* + the *-ed* form is used to show that something happened before a particular point. In the second sentence, the writer goes on with his past-tense narrative.

❖ **Activity 17 Time frames**
Where does the time frame change in these bits of text? What changes in tense are there?

1 I stopped in a lay-by and called Susie Summers. Her father had given me her number, and I checked my note-book and dialled it.

2 I rang a bell and someone buzzed me in. I went to the top floor and worked my way down. People talk to you more willingly when you have a badge to flash.

 Past or present? If you are quoting something that someone has said, it is technically more accurate to use the past tense, for example *said* in *Oscar Wilde **said** that all art is immoral.*

However, the present tense can sound more dynamic if you want to talk about things in literature that are relevant now, for example *Jane Austen **describes** a world that has become familiar to us all.*

You also use the present to report something that is still true, for example *The accused **declares** his innocence.*

It is important, though, that when you change from past to present tense in a story or report, you do it for a reason, to have a particular effect.

Modals

You saw on page 22 that you can use the **modal** *will* to talk about the future. The other important modals are *can, could, would, shall, should, ought to, have to, must, may* and *might*. They are usually followed by an **infinitive** verb form.

Using a modal affects the strength of your statement, showing for example whether you **must** do something or whether you **may** or **might** or **could** do it.

Modals have many different meanings. For example, you can use *can* or *could* to talk about your abilities.

> ▸ Not everyone **can afford** a computer. I certainly **can't**.
> ▸ He didn't think he **could write** any more songs.

You use *should*, *ought to*, *have to* and *must* to talk about what someone advises you to do or what someone tells you to do, particularly someone in authority.

> ▸ I still think you **should tell** your parents.
> ▸ A robot **must obey** the orders given to it by human beings.

You can use *shall* to make a suggestion or an offer, and *could* to make a request.

> ▸ **Shall** I **bring** some lunch up here?
> ▸ **Could** you **unload** the dishwasher and **empty** the rubbish please.

You can use *may*, *might* and *could* to talk about possibilities.

> ▸ A good browse in the library **may give** you some ideas.
> ▸ There are fears that tensions **could lead** to a new war.

The negative of modals is usually formed by adding *not*, or the contraction *n't*.

> ▸ I **couldn't fall** asleep until after midnight.

Only *have to* is different: you say *I have to leave* and *I **don't** have to leave*, as with ordinary verbs.

❖ **Activity 18 Modals**
Fill in the gaps using modals. Use negatives if necessary.

1 You _____ take anything for granted in this life.

2 Here are some ideas that you _____ like to try out.

3 Dave missed the exit so we _____ go round the roundabout again.

4 Is there anything else that I _____ know about?

5 It says on the box that if the seal is broken, you _____ eat them.

Punctuation: Remember that when you use **contractions** of modals, you must put in an apostrophe: *can't, won't, mustn't* etc. This is true for all contractions – **never** forget the apostrophe!

Active and passive

Verbs can be either **active** (*I helped her*) or **passive** (*I was helped*). This is **active**:

> Giant flightless birds *lay* the biggest eggs.

Here the **subject** (the 'doer' of an action) is *giant flightless birds*, and the **object** (the person or thing the action is 'done to') is *the biggest eggs*. The next example is **passive**:

> The biggest eggs *are laid* by giant flightless birds.

The **subject** of the passive sentence is the 'done-to' (*the biggest eggs*), which was the object in the active sentence.

You form the passive using the **auxiliary** *be* in the right form and tense, plus the *-ed* form of a verb. Together they make a passive verb chain.

The first example below is in the present tense (*are*) and the second is in the past (*were*). The form of the main verb stays the same.

> Most acorns *are eaten* by animals.

▸ The first modern Olympics **were held** in Athens in 1896.

You can also use **modals** in passive verb chains.
▸ The match **can't be cancelled** at this late stage.

❖ **Activity 19 The passive – mixed tenses**
Fill in the gaps using the auxiliaries below to make passive verb chains.

was   were   should be   has been   are   can be

1 Their whole crop _____ **destroyed** by elephants last year.

2 All your files _____ **backed up** regularly.

3 The cliffs _____ **formed** when the sea level was higher.

4 The country _____ **ruled** by dictators for decades.

5 We _____ **not allowed** to bring food into the classroom.

6 A lot _____ **achieved** if we set our minds to it.

You choose active or passive according to what your sentence is about
– what the **topic** is. Look at these examples:
▸ People **wore** high-heeled shoes as far back as the sixteenth century.
▸ High-heeled shoes **were worn** as far back as the sixteenth century.

The first sentence is about what *people* did, and the second is about *high-heeled shoes*.

The main difference is that when you use the passive you don't have to
say who did or thought or said something. This may be because you don't
know, or you don't care, or it's people in general, or it doesn't matter. (Or
maybe you don't want to say it was you!)

Verbs

❖ **Activity 20 Why choose the passive?**
Why do you think these writers chose passive verbs?

1 The first bread *was* probably *made* from wild grasses long before wheat *was cultivated*.

2 Every shop and restaurant *is air-conditioned*. You step inside and the sweat *is freeze-dried* on your arms.

What are the subjects of these sentences?

❖ **Activity 21 Why choose the active?**
Why do you think this writer chose active verbs?

Way down south where bananas *grow*,
A grasshopper *stepped* on an elephant's toe.
The elephant *said*, with tears in his eyes,
Pick on somebody your own size.
(anon)

But the 'doer' may still be important, and writers often focus on them at the end of the sentence, which is the most normal position in English for new and important information.

You can introduce them using the **preposition** *by*.

▸ Ishtar *was worshipped* as the goddess of love and war *by the Babylonians, Sumerians and Assyrians.*

Here the 'doers' are clearly crucial to the meaning, while *Ishtar* is the passive, 'done-to' subject. Without *by...* there is not enough information in the sentence.

The passive is used a lot in certain kinds of writing, such as science writing, when you are concentrating on a **process**, not who carried it out.

▸ The metal *was heated* to about 200°C, at which point it began to change colour.

The infinitive

The **infinitive** is the simplest form of the verb without any endings or changes, like *go, come, see, eat* and *wait*. Sometimes it is used with *to*, as in *to eat*.

Without *to*, you use it with *do, does* and *did* (see page 17), and you use it after **modals** (see page 24).

> *Did* you **forget** to turn the radio off?
> I *can* **remember** everything she said.

With *to*, you often use it after other verbs:

> I *forgot* **to bring** the keys.
> I'*m trying* **to concentrate**.

❖ **Activity 22 Verb + *to*-infinitive**
Match the two halves of the sentences.

1 The prime minister refused   **a** to get his parents' permission.

2 She managed   **b** to tell the truth.

3 He remembered   **c** to lose consciousness.

4 I cannot begin   **d** to comment further.

5 I promise   **e** to get a job as a gardener.

6 I'm afraid she's starting   **f** to understand any of this.

The imperative

The **imperative** is also the simplest form of the verb, like the infinitive. You use it to give instructions or commands. The shortest sentence of all consists of just an imperative, but some commands can be much longer.

> **Stop**!
> **Stop** it!
> **Stop** the war!
> **Stop** acting like a spoilt child.
> **Stop** me if you've heard this one before.

Verbs

The imperative is used for instructions, and you will find it a lot in manuals and on packaging. Recipe books, especially, contain a lot of imperatives.

For the negative you use *do not* or the contraction *don't*.

 ▸ **Don't add** the cream until the last minute.
 ▸ **Don't use** biological detergent for your baby's clothes.

❖ **Activity 23 Imperatives**
Match the two halves of the imperative sentences.

1	Vote	**a**	the animals.
2	Watch	**b**	this substance in an enclosed area.
3	Don't feed	**c**	more water.
4	Drink	**d**	this space.
5	Do not spray	**e**	Lib Dem.

Adjectives

The work that adjectives do

The basic job that adjectives do is to give extra information about a noun. They do this in two main ways.

Some of them tell you about the **qualities** of a person or thing – big or small, nice or nasty, interesting or boring. In other words, they give your **opinion** of something. Some people call these 'describing' words, but that is very vague.

a **fantastic** day   a **tasty** meal   a **minor** earthquake
that **dreadful** smell   his **dirty** socks   my **tiny** garden

Others tell you the **kind** of person or thing someone is talking about – male or female, conservative or socialist, urban or rural. These are often called **classifying** adjectives (from the word *class*).

a **female** president   **diplomatic** links   **global** catastrophe
a **national** scandal   **criminal** activities   **electronic** equipment
French politics   **live** music   a **daily** allowance

CAT ADJECTIVES

Adjectives

❖ **Activity 24 Two types of adjective**
Fill in the gaps using the adjectives below.

> **magical   ancient   private   exciting
> secretive   electric   main   utter   new   complete**

1 The _____ Egyptians wore bracelets with _____ charms dangling from them.

2 She said a bit about her_____ _____ band, then strapped on an_____ guitar.

3 During this time, my _____ symptom was _____ and _____ exhaustion.

4 Tanya is very _____ , and doesn't like anyone to interfere in her _____ life.

The **colours** are also adjectives. They can be nouns as well (see page 9), but they are more often adjectives.

*a **black** cat*   *a **green** dress*   *a **red** sky*

The *-ing* and *-ed* forms of many verbs can also be used as adjectives.

▶ Our society has ***increasing*** numbers of old people.
▶ The Chinese made ***printed*** books as long ago as the sixth century.

The position of adjectives

You can use adjectives:

■ before a noun
■ after a verb like *be* or *seem*

▶ It's a very ***clean*** factory.
▶ Some snakes *are **poisonous***.
▶ Your argument *seems **reasonable***.

The classifying adjectives are more often used before a noun.

▶ She seems to be in ***financial*** trouble.
▶ This is a ***national*** scandal.

Adjective order

When you have more than one adjective before a noun, the 'opinion' ones usually come first, then the colour adjectives, then the classifying adjectives. This is not a hard-and-fast rule, and sometimes a different order 'sounds' better.

▸ Pavel was wearing a ***scruffy red military*** cap.
▸ She had ***lovely black spiky*** hair.
▸ Cheong was driving a ***huge**, **white**, **convertible*** car.

 Punctuation: Note that sometimes you put commas between adjectives when you use more than one of them. There is not a strict rule, so do what looks and sounds best.

If you want to give more detail about a colour, you can use words like *bright*, *light*, *pale* and *dark* before the adjective.

▸ I hated that ***bright yellow chewy*** fish you served up last night.

❖ **Activity 25   Adjective order**
Put the adjectives in brackets into their most natural order before the noun.

1 Bathed in _____ light, they sat staring at the TV. (fluorescent sickly green)

2 Today she wore _____ cotton. (Indian blue pale cool)

3 Meena went out and bought a _____ bubble dress. (chiffon silly purple)

Comparative adjectives

You use comparative adjectives to compare two people, things or situations.

Forms

Some adjectives have **comparative** forms. (They also have **superlative** forms – see page 37.)

Adjectives

You form the **comparative** by adding *-er* or *-ier*.

clean → clean**er**	plain → plain**er**
soft → soft**er**	small → small**er**
dirty → dirt**ier**	happy → happ**ier**

But you can't add *-er* to longer adjectives. You use *more* (or *less*) instead, and the form of the adjective does not change.

interesting → **more** interesting	famous → **more** famous
frequent → **less** frequent	accurate → **less** accurate

 Standard and non-standard: Be careful not to use 'double comparatives' like

X *more prettier*

X *less friendlier*

You either add *-er* or use *more*, **not both**.

✓ *prettier, more pretty*

✓ *friendlier, less friendly*

Also be careful not to use *more* with most short adjectives:

X *more large*

✓ *larger, smaller*

There are a few **irregular** comparative forms:

good → **better**
bad → **worse**
far → **further** / **farther**

Uses

You often use comparatives to compare a situation with what things were like before.

> ▸ Plants are blooming *earlier* and *earlier*, largely because of the *warmer* global climate.
> ▸ The work seems to be getting *more* and *more difficult*.

▶ I found it hard to deal with the pain. So I ignored it, and it got **worse**.

When you want to compare two things in a very clear way, you can use *than*.
▶ Primate males are **more aggressive** *than* females.
▶ He knew he sounded a lot **more cheerful** *than* he felt.
▶ At Forest Hill the children are receiving more attention from teachers *than* at **more crowded** schools.

 Standard and non-standard: The things you compare using *than* should be similar. For example, you shouldn't say

✗ *The weather in England is warmer than Norway.*

Weather and *Norway* are not the same sort of thing. You could say instead

✓ *The weather in England is warmer than **it is** in Norway.*

❖ **Activity 26 Comparative adjectives (1)**
Put the words in the right order to make sentences. The first word(s) is in the right place.

Example:

Crocodiles / than / alligators / more aggressive / are

Crocodiles are more aggressive than alligators.

1 Diesel / more fuel-efficient / engines / engines / are / thirty percent / than / petrol

2 The animals / the zoo / from / were moved / ground / higher / to

3 He / spaghetti / more adventurous / rarely / than / bolognese / cooked / anything

4 Barbecues / ever / now / than / more popular / are

5 Since 2000, / fashion / more and / has become / more accessible / people / to

6 The new / is going to be / and / better / the last / than / show / bigger

Adjectives

❖ **Activity 27 Comparative adjectives (2)**
Fill in the gaps using the adjectives below. Which two adjectives could be used in more than one place?

bigger   flatter   smaller   larger   rounder   less prominent

Over the past two million years, human skulls have gradually got a _____ face, _____ teeth, and a _____ jaw. The top of the skull has become _____ and _____ , to house the _____ brain.

Emphasizing a comparison

When you want to emphasize the size of the difference between two things, you can use words like *slightly*, *a little*, *much*, *far* and *a lot*. If you took these words out of the next examples, the effect on your reader would be less strong and clear.

▶ There must be *far* **more effective** ways of cutting crime than locking people up for years.

▶ I seem to be *a lot* **busier** than ever these days.

▶ She wants to have her baby at home because it's *much* **more natural**, she says.

▶ Let's go upstairs. It might be *a little* **less crowded** up there.

You can also use *even* or *still* for emphasis.

▶ The kokoi is *even* **more poisonous** than the arrow-poison frog.

❖ **Activity 28 Emphasizing a comparison**
Complete the lists 1 and 2 with the words below, so that you have two lists of words with similar meanings.

**infinitely   marginally   a bit   a good deal
a great deal   considerably   vastly**

1 far, much, a lot, _____ , _____ , _____ , _____ ,
_____

2 slightly, a little, _____ , _____

36

Now put a word from either the first or the second list into the right place in these sentences. Do some fit better than others?

1 The mass of the Sun is larger than that of the Earth.

2 Her share of the vote was higher than her rival's – 30.1 per cent compared with 29.8.

3 Even the store's luxury breakfast was only £3.25 – cheaper than Tinto's at £5.95.

4 Victoria has suffered its second driest decade on record , with the drought of 1935–45 only worse.

Superlative adjectives

You use the superlative to say that a person or thing is bigger or better or more interesting than **anything else** at a particular time or in a particular place. You form the **superlative** by adding -*est* or -*iest* to an adjective, usually putting *the* before it as well.

clean → **the clean**est   *plain* → **the plain**est
soft → **the soft**est   *small* → **the small**est
dirty → **the dirt**iest   *happy* → **the happ**iest

But just as in the case of comparatives, you can't add -*est* to longer adjectives. You add *the most* (or *the least*) instead, and the form of the adjective does not change.

interesting → **the most interesting**   *famous* → **the most famous**
frequent → **the least frequent**   *accurate* → **the least accurate**

The irregular ones are

good → (*better*) → **the best**
bad → (*worse*) → **the worst**
far → (*further*) → **the furthest** / **the farthest**

Typical phrases that occur with superlatives are *in the world*, *in the country*, *I've ever seen*, *ever* and *possible*.

▸ He has **the most beautiful** green eyes *you've ever seen*.
▸ I thought she might die. It was **the most distressing** situation *possible*.

Adjectives

▶ Ludwig Wittgenstein was **the ablest** logician *of his time*.
▶ Compared to other positions, offensive linemen are **the beefiest** players *on the field*.

> *Most* + adjective, without *the*, often means the same as *very*, as in *Thank you, that was **most interesting***. This does not mean 'more interesting than anything else'.

❖ **Activity 29 Superlative adjectives**
Put the words in the right order to make sentences. The first word(s) is/are in the right place.

1 Each day / selections / in our blog / we / World Cup / the best / will present

2 According to / New York City / the most / on / courteous·/ a new survey, /the planet / place / is

3 Childhood / most / of / human development / vital / the / is / part

4 The / biggest game / the / in / history /Australian / match / is

5 I'm / she's / not the most / world / the / mother / responsible / afraid / in

❖ **Activity 30 Comparatives and superlatives**
Fill in the gaps using a comparative or superlative form of the adjective in brackets. (Two of the adjectives have two possible forms.)

1 He had walked a much _____ distance than he had intended. (long)

2 The café was very gloomy. I could see why the only customer had chosen to sit in _____ corner. (far)

3 They were discussing who was _____ choice from the twelve candidates. (likely)

4 She was nice enough to begin with, but became even _____ when I slipped her a twenty. (helpful)

5 I ate at the Fat Pheasant – not _____ food in the world, or even in Slough. (great)

6 Australia are _____ in one-day cricket than in Test Matches. (vulnerable)

Saying that things are similar

You may also want to say that two things or people are the same or similar in some way, or that a situation is the same as before. For this you can use *as...* or *as...as...* . To point out a difference, you can say *not as...* .

> Like us, the French love football, but the fans just are**n't** as **obsessive**.
> The throbbing pain in my head is not as **bad** as it was, but it's still there.

 The structure *as ... as ...* is often used in **similes**, where one thing is described as being like another. This creates a vivid picture:

*The place was **as** noisy **as** a classroom before the teacher arrives.*

Using adjectives to add detail and precision

Writers use adjectives to add detail and precision to what they are saying, and to make what they are describing more interesting and real to the reader.

 Writing that contains adjectives is sure to be more interesting than if you just use one bare noun after another. But too many adjectives make a narrative look 'over-written' and may slow the action down or clutter up a description.

? A beautiful, glamorous, elegant, famous celebrity was flashing her even, white, perfect teeth at her silent, hushed, worshipping fans in the luxurious wood-panelled hotel lobby.

Adjectives

❖ **Activity 31 Adjectives for detail and precision**

Most of the adjectives have been taken out of this passage. Read it first, covering up the gapped version below. Discuss which adjectives you would add and where. Then fill in the second version, using **all** the adjectives given at the bottom. Which version do you prefer?

The creature let out a roar. I stumbled, and fell at the feet of a man, who stared at the creature. I had an impression of his features. He had a beard around his chin, white eyebrows, and glasses.

The _____ creature let out a _____ roar. I stumbled, and fell at the feet of a _____ man, who stared at the creature. I had a _____ impression of his features. He had a _____ beard around his chin, _____ white eyebrows, and _____ glasses.

> **loud   bushy   bear-like   fleeting   small**
> **elderly   stubby   white   corrective**

Variation: Look at the **preposition** *toward* in the first line. This tells you that the writer of the sci-fi book that the passage comes from is American. In British English, you use *towards*.

Adverbs

The work that adverbs do

The basic job that adverbs do is to give extra information, usually about a verb, but sometimes about an adjective or about a whole **clause** (see Part 4, page 120). There are several ways in which they do this, so there are several kinds of adverb. These are just a few of them.

Types of adverb

Manner adverbs

These are the most 'typical' kinds of adverb – they give you information about a verb by telling you **how** something happens or is done. They are usually formed from adjectives by adding *-ly*.

quiet → *quiet**ly***   *beautiful* → *beautiful**ly***
accurate → *accurate**ly***   *clumsy* → *clums**ily***

> ▸ The government has failed to spend the money **sensibly**.
> ▸ Tagrid was eating **steadily**, as if to make up for many lost meals.
> ▸ He's a good defensive infielder, but he's never hit **consistently**.

He ate adverbially!

41

Adverbs

Well is an **irregular** adverb related to *good*, and *hard* and *fast* are adverbs as well as adjectives.

> She hates driving **fast**.

 Standard and non-standard: Some people think that you shouldn't use *quick* as an adverb (instead of *quickly*), as in

> *? Oh, the biscuits are going quick – I'd better have one.*

But the English language is changing, and this use of *quick* may be becoming acceptable. At present your teacher would probably consider it wrong.

❖ **Activity 32 Adverbs and adjectives**
Fill in the gaps using the words below. One of each pair is an adjective and the other an adverb.

**helpless/helplessly   dangerous/dangerously
good/well   brilliant/brilliantly**

1 He stamped his feet in _____ frustration.

2 Good for you – you dealt with the whole problem very _____ .

3 'Ron,' I said _____. 'Save me. Do something.'

4 And Mrs Wilson here is rather _____ at making pastry.

5 Can too many vitamins be _____ ?

6 My team-mates have been _____ and a lot of fans are proud of what I've achieved.

7 Premiership clubs are flirting _____ with bankruptcy.

8 The pressure is on but it's all turned out _____ for the team.

Like the adjectives they come from, manner adverbs usually have **comparative** and **superlative** forms. To form the comparative, add *more*, and to form the superlative, add *most* or *the most*.

> A can of paint will freshen up a room **more quickly** than any other option.

▸ It is the poorest people who will feel the price rise **most acutely**.

The adjectives *hard* and *fast* are also adverbs. They add *-er* to make the comparative, and *-est* to make the superlative.
  ▸ I'm determined to work **harder**.
  ▸ We'll see who can run the **fastest**.

The **irregular** comparative adjectives *better* and *best*, *worse* and *worst* are also adverbs.
  ▸ I felt I rode **better** than ever last year.
  ▸ Let's see who can do it **best**.

Time adverbs

You can talk about time in different ways, using adverbs like *instantly*, *shortly*, *soon*, *later*, *afterwards*, and *suddenly*.
  ▸ Brown under the grill for about five minutes, then serve **immediately**.
  ▸ Penalties will include suspension and **eventually** a one-year ban from the sport.

Other time adverbs, like *frequently*, *sometimes* and *rarely* are used to say **how often** something happens. Adverbs like *briefly*, *temporarily*, *indefinitely* and *permanently* are used to say **how long** something goes on.
  ▸ He had his own television, but he **rarely** switched it on these days.
  ▸ Add the carrots and cook for 10–15 minutes, stirring **occasionally**.
  ▸ David has now been barred from the sport **indefinitely**.

Place adverbs

There are a lot of adverbs you can use to talk about **where** someone or something is, or in what **position**. A few of these are *here, there, everywhere, nearby, away, ahead, outdoors, abroad, upstairs, underground, northwards* and *inland*.
  ▸ In 1969 we at last had our own bathroom and toilet, **indoors**.
  ▸ Sue made her way unsteadily **downstairs**, holding onto my arm.
  ▸ I can swim a whole length **underwater**.

Adverbs

❖ **Activity 33 Time and place adverbs**
Match the questions with their answers.

1	'Which direction is the coast?'	**a**	'**Later**, perhaps.'
2	'Do you go to the gym?'	**b**	'I don't know. Maybe **never**.'
3	'Where would you like to sit?'	**c**	'**Temporarily**, yes.'
4	'Would you like a shower?'	**d**	'**Outdoors**, preferably.'
5	'When will he be released?'	**e**	'**Sometimes. Not enough**.'
6	'Are you working these days?'	**f**	'**Eastwards**, I think.'

Aspect adverbs

There is a very useful group of adverbs that you can use to make it clear **which angle** you are speaking from. Some common ones are:

economically	biologically	commercially
culturally	ecologically	socially
physically	mentally	psychologically
politically	financially	emotionally

- ▸ I'm sure our plan is **ecologically** sound.
- ▸ War damages a country both **politically** and **economically**.
- ▸ **Psychologically**, many smokers find it hard to give up.
- ▸ Wind power is becoming **financially** attractive.

Sentence adverbs

Some adverbs can be used to link sentences together. The most useful of these are *moreover, however, even so, nevertheless* and *therefore*.

- ▸ Salim had no idea how the pieces of the puzzle fitted together. **However**, he was glad that Anna was there to talk it through with him.

These adverbs are also called **connectives**, and are dealt with more fully in Part 5, pages 152–4.

44

Degree adverbs

There is an important group of adverbs that you use to emphasize your description of a quality or process. They have a strong effect on your reader because they show that you really mean what you say. For example, if you tell someone that you *totally* agree with them, this is more positive and supportive than just saying that you agree. Here is a list of some useful degree adverbs:

completely	*truly*	*entirely*
fully	*simply*	*outright*
quite	*virtually*	*utterly*
totally	*absolutely*	*purely*
perfectly	*really*	*positively*

You often put these before an adjective to give extra emphasis, but they can come in other positions as well, before or after a verb for example.

▸ It is now ***virtually*** *impossible* for unskilled workers to come here legally.

▸ Governments are ***simply*** *incapable* of knowing which workers are needed where.

▸ I'm ***quite*** *happy* to listen to what you have to say.

▸ By the time he left, the city *had changed* ***utterly***.

There is also a large group of adverbs of degree that you can put before adjectives to say **how much** of a quality something has. Some of these are:

extremely	*terribly*	*incredibly*
remarkably	*enormously*	*very*
exceptionally	*so*	*fairly*
quite	*rather*	*somewhat*
relatively	*moderately*	*slightly*

▸ These days, submarines are ***relatively*** *easy* and *cheap* to build.

▸ She admitted that she was ***slightly*** *anxious* about leaving Sydney.

▸ Heat the olive oil over a ***moderately*** *high* heat in a shallow casserole.

▸ Tamil Nadu has received ***exceptionally*** *heavy* rains in the north-east monsoon.

> **Our changing language:** Some people think it is wrong to use *well* before an adjective – *He sounds **well** <u>angry</u> and wants to speak to the manager.* With other adjectives, however, it sounds quite normal and natural:
>
> *I am **well** <u>aware</u> of the risks involved.*
>
> So there seems no reason not to use it before any adjective, if you like to be creative.

Note that you do not usually use degree adverbs before classifying adjectives (see page 32). You can't say ✗ *very electronic* or ✗ *quite female*.

❖ **Activity 34 Degree adverbs**
Match each adverb with an adjective, according to what sounds most natural to you.

1	remarkably	**a**	sorry
2	utterly	**b**	surprising
3	somewhat	**c**	useless
4	fully	**d**	similar
5	terribly	**e**	fit

You can put the same adverbs before other *adverbs*, here a manner adverb.
▸ *'I can't answer that,' he said **somewhat** apologetically.*

Phrasal verbs (verb-adverb combinations)

There is also a small group of adverbs that are used after certain verbs. The most common of these are *on, off, in, out, up, down, along, back* and *over*. The verb and the adverb together form a verb with a particular meaning. These are often called **phrasal verbs**. Some examples are:

fall **over**	set **in**	catch **on**
grow **up**	find **out**	turn **down**
switch **off**	put **away**	pay **back**

▸ The problem is that after a time, boredom and apathy *set in*.

▸ I will need to *find **out*** exactly what the problem is.

▸ She made me *put* all my books ***away***.

Note that these adverbs are different from the other adverbs discussed above because they are a **closed class**, and very similar to prepositions.

❖ **Activity 35 Phrasal verbs**
All these sentences contain phrasal verbs. Fill in the gaps using the right adverbs.

1 Steam and ashes filled the room as the stew **boiled** _____ into the fire, putting it out.

2 If they borrow something and **give** it _____ damaged, they have to pay for the damage caused.

3 The vaccine's effectiveness **wears** _____ over time.

4 She **wrote** something _____ , but then immediately **crossed** it _____ .

5 I'm afraid you've **left** _____ the most important point.

Other adverbs

As well as those already mentioned, there are many other types of adverb. The class as a whole is very varied, and is often referred to as a 'rag-bag' class. This means that if a word doesn't fit easily into any class, the chances are it's an adverb.

Just, for example, is a common adverb that is unlike any other. In these sentences it means 'only', 'recently', 'at that moment', 'exactly' and 'simply'.

▸ What were the chances that this was ***just*** a coincidence?

▸ I ***just*** had a terrible dream.

▸ When he awoke the train was ***just*** beginning to move.

▸ This creature was ***just*** like the other one – a fishy, reptilian thing.

▸ I ***just*** can't understand anything!

Adverbs

❖ **Activity 36 Another very common adverb**
Which little adverb can you put into all these sentences?

1 Luckily , he had _____ to see the giant spider who had built this atrocious trap.

2 The roof was sagging but hadn't _____ collapsed inwards.

3 I raised my eyes to heaven _____ again.

4 We need to build two big bonfires – or better _____ , fireworks displays.

The position of adverbs

You usually put manner adverbs after a verb, but you can put them at the beginning of the sentence for emphasis.

▸ He drove *carefully*, checking the street signs.
▸ *Carefully*, I brushed away the layer of dust that covered the scroll.

Many adverbs can also go before the **main verb**, or between the auxiliary and the main verb.

▸ I've noticed that animals *often* empathize with children.
▸ I've *never* forgotten what happened that day.

Many degree adverbs go before an **adjective**.

▸ It was obvious that things were going *drastically* wrong.
▸ He set a new standard for being *totally* and *utterly* selfish.

> **Our changing language:** People used to say (and some still do) that it is wrong to 'split an infinitive' by putting an adverb in the middle, as in the famous opening of *Star Trek*, 'to boldly go where no man has gone before'. But teachers now consider it acceptable to use an adverb in this position, especially when it sounds the most natural.

Using adverbs to add detail and precision

You can use adverbs to add detail and precision, in much the same way as you use adjectives.

❖ **Activity 37 Adverbs for detail and precision**

Most of the adverbs have been taken out of these sentences. Read them first, covering up the gapped version below. Discuss which adverbs you would add and where. Then fill in the second version, using the adverbs given at the bottom. Which version do you prefer?

1 **'Listen, I'll get the key!' She repeated the words. 'I'll get the key and I'll come back!'**

2 **He went to his lonely bed in the other room and fell asleep. He stirred and then sat up, wondering why it was light.**

3 **Her bereaved parents spoke about a daughter who had spent her life caring for disabled people.**

1 'Listen, I'll get the key!' She repeated the words _____ and _____ . 'I'll get the key and I'll come back!'

2 He went _____ to his lonely bed in the other room and _____ fell asleep. _____ he stirred _____ and then sat up, wondering why it was _____ light.

3 Her bereaved parents spoke _____ about a daughter who had spent her life caring for _____ and _____ disabled people.

> **quietly   distinctly   physically   quickly   presently
> mentally   tearfully   uneasily   clearly   so**

Can you identify the **phrasal verbs** in these sentences?

Word class: the grammatical classes

Part 2

Conjunctions

Pronouns

The work that pronouns do

Pronouns are little words like *she, it, me, them, mine, ours, myself, this* and *those*. They stand alone, and can be, for example, the subject or object of a sentence. Many of them fall into other classes as well.

Pronouns are a **closed class**. This means that no new ones can be added, though people are always trying to invent them (see pages 55–56 and 59).

The most typical thing that pronouns do is to 'stand in' for a noun that has been used before. Using a pronoun means that you do not have to repeat the noun. In these examples, the <u>underlined</u> words show you what the pronoun is standing in for.

> ▶ <u>Maya</u> understood. ***She*** deliberated for a moment.
> ▶ Billy dropped <u>the bones</u> and carefully ground ***them*** into the sand with his shoe.
> ▶ Then <u>his mother</u> was standing up and trying to make ***herself*** heard above the crowd.

❖ **Activity 1   What pronouns refer back to**

Underline the person or thing that the pronouns in **bold** are referring back to.

1 I wondered if I was seeing the same things through my eyes that everyone else was seeing through **theirs**.

2 You are not going over to Reem's house. **She** can come here instead.

3 Constanza pointed both her index fingers towards **herself** – 'movie star!'

4 Most reports of apparent mystical powers are crude and patently false. I ignore **those**.

5 Every time Sid opened his mouth, **he** put his foot in **it**.

Sometimes, however, pronouns don't seem to be 'standing in' for anyone or anything. The pronoun *it* in these sentences just acts as an 'empty' subject.

> ▸ *It*'s all right – we can walk from here.
> ▸ *It*'s just that I can read your thoughts.
> ▸ *It*'s really windy outside.
> ▸ Soon *it* was raining torrents and we all fled into the hut.

Types of pronoun

There are many different types of pronoun, and some of them look the same or almost the same.

Personal pronouns

These pronouns can be grouped according to **person**. The **first person** pronouns are *I* and *me, we* and *us.* They identify the speaker or speakers.

There is only one **second person** pronoun – *you,* which is used to identify the person or people being spoken to, whether they are the subject or object of the clause.

The **third person** pronouns are *he* and *him, she* and *her, it they* and *them.* These refer to the people or things being spoken about.

 If you are describing a personal experience, you are likely to use a **first person narrator** and the forms *I, me,* etc. This makes your writing or talk seem direct and heartfelt.

When you are writing a story, you can also use *I* and *me,* but you could choose to tell the story in the **third person**, using *he, she, Jenny* etc. When you choose a third person narrator, you need to decide how to express your characters' thoughts and feelings – from the point of view of just one of them, or as if you can 'get into the heads' of all of them.

Pronouns can also be grouped into two other sets – **subject** and **object pronouns**.

One set consists of *I, you, he, she, it, we* and *they. You* is both singular and plural. All these pronouns can be the **subject** of a sentence (the 'doer', the person responsible for a situation etc).

▸ **She** didn't even know his name.

The verb must agree with the pronoun you use.

✓ **They** *admire* him, but **they** *are* afraid **he** *is* too inexperienced to compete.

✗ They admires him, but they is afraid he are too inexperienced to compete.

The other set of personal pronouns consists of *me, you, him, her, it, us* and *them*. All these pronouns can be the **object** (the person or thing an action is 'done to'). You also use them after **prepositions** like *to* and *for*.

▸ We ought to go and help **him**.

▸ We've arranged everything. Just leave it all *to **us***.

❖ **Activity 2 Personal pronouns**
Fill in the gaps using the pronouns below.

they   they   she   he   him

1 The police have released _____ , saying _____ do not believe _____ is much of a threat.

2 'We know that people will have different reactions,' _____ says. 'And we hope _____ all do the right thing.'

Avoiding sexist pronouns: Did you know that in English we have no **gender-neutral** pronouns? This means that we have no pronoun that refers to either a man or a woman.

Women especially often object to *he* being used in sentences like this, since an *Australian supporter* could be either male or female:

*Ask any Australian supporter if **he** would prefer to see a hard-fought contest, or a walkover.*

You should definitely avoid this in your writing.

At various times people have invented and used gender-neutral pronouns, for example ***sie*** for *he* and *she*, and ***hir*** for *him* and *her*. But these didn't catch on, and the best we can do is *he or she*, or *s/he*.

> *Observe a Parisian driver when **he or she** comes up against a red light.*
> *A child needs all the careers advice **s/he** can get.*

It is also acceptable to use *they* or *them* when you are referring to a single unspecified person. Look at these examples:

> *Everybody should marry as soon as **they** can do it to advantage.* (Jane Austen)
> *If someone blacks out, **they** become unconscious for a short time.* (dictionary definition)
> *If anyone got into trouble, we always supported **them**.*
> *Experience is the name everyone gives to **their** mistakes.* (Oscar Wilde)

In your writing, you can sometimes avoid the problem by making the whole sentence plural.

> *We may damage a child by labelling **him or her** as a failure.*
> → *We may damage children by labelling **them** as failures.*

❖ **Activity 3 Avoiding sexist pronouns**
Find ways of avoiding sexist language by rewriting the sentences.

1 If a thief steals your card, he cannot access your personal account.

2 Each person has a DNA profile that is unique to him.

 Standard and non-standard: In Liverpool, Manchester and some parts of Scotland and Ireland, *yous* (often spelt *youse*) is often used instead of *you* when addressing people.

> *It's dead secret and I'm only telling **yous** because you're good mates.*

You should not use this in your writing.

You can use the pronoun *you* as subject or object to mean *anyone*.
▸ When **you** reach rock-bottom, the only way to go is up.

Finally, you can use *one* as a personal pronoun, again to mean *anyone*, though this is rather formal. Members of the royal family seem to use it freely to mean *I* or *me*.

▸ ***One*** does not have to be thin to be healthy.
▸ ***One*** does find such sights rather distasteful.

Using the right personal pronoun

The main problem that people have with pronouns is knowing which one to use.

 Standard and non-standard: Is it *Tom **and I*** or *Tom **and me***? The general rule is that you do the same as when you use *I* and *me* alone – for the subject you use *I*, and for the object, or after a preposition like *for*, you use *me*.

> ***Alena and I*** *have a master plan.* (subject)
> *Many people have contacted **Deborah and me** asking about the campaign.* (object)
> *I'll cook these sausages for **Daddy and me**.* (after preposition)

You use the same rule with the subject pronouns *he*, *she*, *we* and *they* and the object pronouns *him*, *her*, *us* and *them*.

> *Why did **Jon and she** split up?* (subject)
> *The situation is upsetting **him and us**.* (object)

But in conversation and informal situations, many people increasingly use *me* for the subject pronoun. This is also typical of many non-standard dialects.

> ⁊ *There was a time when **Charlotte, my Den and me** used to go around together.* (subject)

Often, too, people put *me* first.

> ⁊ ***Me and your mum*** *get along fine.*

You should not use this in your writing.

Be careful not to overcorrect. Some people think that *I* is somehow more grammatical than *me*, especially after the preposition *between*. You should use *me* here.

> ✗ *The word 'ghost' was never mentioned between Naim and I.*

> ✓ *The word 'ghost' was never mentioned between **Naim and me**.*

Our changing language: In the sentences below you can use the subject pronouns *I, we, they* etc. This used to be the 'rule'.

> *This time it was **I** who had the last word.*
> *It was **he** who did most of the planning.*
> *It is **we** who are unwilling to make peace.*

But a lot of people use the object pronouns *me, us, them* etc instead, and this is getting more common.

> *It was **me** who went looking for her.*
> *It was **him** who leaked the story.*
> *Unfortunately it was **us** who made the mistake.*

Which of the sets of sentences would you be more likely to say?

Which of the sentences below would you use?

> *He's a better man **than I**.*
> *A lot of players are better **than me**.*
> *She's much more mature **than I am**.*

Not many people would use the first one nowadays, though in the past it was thought more correct than the second.

Possessive pronouns

The possessive pronouns are *mine, yours, his, hers, ours* and *theirs*. You use them to indicate that something belongs to someone or is connected with them in some way.

> ▸ I will give you the power that should be ***yours.***

You often use these pronouns to compare two things that are associated with different people. You do not need to repeat the noun – in the next example you do not need to say *I can hardly breathe in my dress*, because it is obvious.

> ▸ What *a lovely dress*! I can hardly breathe in ***mine***, it's so tight.
> ▸ The beast was only a few yards away. *Its eyes* locked with ***hers***.

You can use these pronouns after *of*.

> ▸ Ali and Abdu knew that she was a cousin ***of theirs***.

❖ **Activity 4 Possessive pronouns**
Match the two halves of the sentences.

1 I've always been a great   **a** ambition of mine.

2 Helen is a very good   **b** admirer of hers.

3 Coaching Wales remains a   **c** concern of yours.
   burning

4 Her private life is no   **d** favourite of mine.

5 This album is a particular   **e** friend of mine

Reflexive pronouns

The words *myself, yourself, himself, herself, itself, ourselves, yourselves* and *themselves* are also pronouns. You use these **reflexive pronouns** to refer to a person or thing that is the same as the subject of the sentence.

▸ Somehow *Tim* managed to make ***himself*** understood.

▸ I rolled my eyes but *I* couldn't bring ***myself*** to contradict her aloud.

▸ *We*'ll just have to learn to milk the cows ***ourselves***.

▸ *A grey light* settled ***itself*** with a quick shiver over the landscape.

> **Our changing language:** Remember that closed classes like pronouns are usually quite fixed. But change is happening – as explained on page 56 you can now use *they* and *them* as **gender-neutral pronouns**. It now seems that a new reflexive pronoun, *themself*, is catching on.
>
> > *A person who identifies **themself** as 'Epping Reader' has faxed us.*
> > *Physical appearance is a sign of how someone feels about **themself**.*
>
> Although over 120 sentences using this pronoun can be found in our collection of real language, you should not use it in your writing (yet).
>
> Other different forms, such as *hisself* and *theirselves*, are used in many non-standard dialects, for example in Cornwall and Wales and in African-American English.
>
> You should definitely not use these in your writing either.

Demonstrative pronouns

The demonstrative pronouns are *this, that, these* and *those*. You use them to refer to a person or thing you have mentioned before or that you can see in front of you.

> We are standing by for *the president's news conference.* **That** will come up at the top of the hour.

> '**These** are your children?' Nessie asked, turning to the forester.

You can also use *this* to refer forward to something you are going to say.

> Listen to **this**!

This and *that* often refer back to a statement or a whole situation.

> *He said that the system wasn't working and would have to be scrapped.* **This** is an amazing admission.

Question pronouns

You use the question pronouns *who, whose, whom, what* and *which* to ask questions.

> **Who** was she hiding from?

> '**What** is your name, child?' 'Frith.'

Relative pronouns

The relative pronouns are *who, whom, that* and *which*. They introduce **relative clauses**.

> In Hilaire Belloc's poem, Mathilda was a little girl **who** burned her house down.

> Glaciers are rivers of ice **that** form in cold climates.

 Standard and non-standard: The word *what* is **not** a relative pronoun.

✗ *Maybe if you was to write me another cheque, to make up for the one what got stole?*

You should not use sentences like this in your writing.

See Part 4, pages 135–9 for more information about relative clauses and the relative pronouns they begin with.

'Amount' pronouns

Finally, there is a group of pronouns that refer to a **proportion** or an **amount**. Some of these are *both*, *a few*, *plenty*, *some*, *any* and *enough*.

▸ I handed him a twenty-pound note. 'Will that be **enough**?'

❖ **Activity 5 Pronouns – mixed types**
Put the words in the right order to make sentences. The first word is in the right place.

Example:

He / door / firmly / it / and / walked / closed / the / to

He walked to the door and closed it firmly.

1 Megan / comfortable / herself / the armchair / in / made

2 Their / quite / from / culture / different / is / ours

3 Mr Twit / and / cooked / Mrs Twit / the birds / caught / them

4 I / the ice-cream / some / decided / eat / to / and / looked at

5 Janny / khaki shorts / an old pair / was wearing / of / Robert's / These / enormous / her / looked / on

Reference chains

When you write, you may be using pronouns to refer back to more than one person or thing, and you often use the same pronoun more than once. In this example, there are three chains of pronoun reference:

▸ *The police* wanted **me** for a line-up, to identify *the girl*. **They** wouldn't say why **they**'d arrested **her**, but one of **them** did tell **me** that **he** thought **she** was Polish.

The three reference chains are pronouns standing in for the police (*they*, *they*, *them*, *he*), for the girl (*her*, *she*), and the narrator (*me*, *me*).

You could improve this by using fewer pronouns, for example … *but one of the officers did tell me* …

Pronouns

 Sometimes reference chains get muddled, and you lose track of who is who.

*Mrs Slaski loved her daughter. **She** could not understand why **she** did not want to see **her**, although **she** wanted to stand by **her** during her recovery.*

It is not quite clear whether the second *she* and the first *her* refer to *Mrs Slaski* or *her daughter*. If your reference chain gets muddled, repeat a noun, or better, use a different noun.

*… **She** could not understand why the child did not want to see **her** …*

❖ **Activity 6 Reference chains**
Complete the pronoun chains in the conversation below.

Jack: It's tearing _____ apart to think we're just going to leave your parents but _____ can't see any alternative. Do _____ think they'd understand, Mel?

Mel: _____ would want _____ to do whatever's best for us, Jack. They would want _____ to escape and make a new life for _____ .

Determiners

Determiners are little words that you put at the beginning of a **noun group** to show which person or thing you mean, or to show the quantity of something.

Types and uses of determiners

Articles
The commonest determiners are *the* and *a(n)*. *The* is in fact by far the most frequent word in the English language. *The* is often called the **definite article** and *a(n)* is called the **indefinite article**.

> ▸ I was spending ***the*** *holiday* with ***a*** *friend* in ***a*** *caravan*.
> ▸ We emerged into ***the*** *gray-green light* of ***a*** *cloudy day* in ***the*** *forest*.

> **Variation:** The spelling of *gray-green* in the last example tells you that the writer is American. In British English, the spelling is **grey-green**.

When you use the indefinite article, you use *an* before words beginning with the vowels *a*, *e*, *i*, *o* and *u*, as in *an eagle*.

But when a *u* makes the sound like the consonant *y*, you use *a*. It helps to say these sentences aloud:

> ▸ Billy finds ***an*** *unexpected* ally in life.
> ▸ That's ***a*** *useful* gadget!

You also use *an* before words beginning with *h* when the *h* is silent, as in *an honest girl, an honourable girl*.

Possessives
Some determiners show **possession**. These are *my, your, his, her, its, our* and *their*.

Determiners

▶ He folded **his** arms on the side of **my** bed and rested **his** chin on his arms.
▶ Laughing, the two ghouls raised **their** axes and chopped at **our** piano.

> **Variation:** In some dialects, people use *our* when referring to a family member.
>
> *Have you seen **our** Arthur?*

Demonstratives

This, *that*, *these* and *those* are also determiners. They can refer back to a person or thing you mentioned before, or to a statement or situation.

▶ There was *a large perfumed candle* on the table. **This** candle was rarely lit.
▶ '*Now, raise your weapon and fight.*' With **those** words, Rama pulled back his arrow.

You can use demonstratives to refer to something you can see or hear, or something that you and the person you are talking to both know about.

▶ Let's look through **these** *old papers*.
▶ We could use **that** *big iron pot* in the kitchen.

 Standard and non-standard: *This* and *these* are often used to introduce a person or thing you are going to talk about.

*There was **this** <u>girl</u> I liked who was in the chess class …*

This is quite informal and you should avoid it in your formal writing.

 Standard and non-standard: Note that *them* is **not** a determiner in standard English.

*? How do you like **them** apples?*

*✓ How do you like **those** apples?*

Amounts

You use many other determiners to specify a vague or specific **proportion** or **amount**. They can be grouped like this:

100 per cent	*all, each, every*
a large number or amount	*much, many, most, several*
some	*some, any*
a small number or amount	*a few, a little, few, little*
two	*both, either*
one more	*another*
none	*neither* (of two), *no*

> ▹ Arash was wearing a big floppy hat, **several** sizes too large.
> ▹ I'm afraid I have **some** bad news for you.
> ▹ The windscreens of **both** cars had shattered in the crash.
> ▹ There's **no** need for you to feel guilty.

Enough is also a determiner and so are *more, less* and *fewer*.

> ▹ We cyclists are not given **enough** space!
> ▹ For **more** information, visit our website.

 Less or **fewer**? You should use *fewer* with a **plural count noun**. Many people wrongly use *less* instead, and this is becoming more frequent, but you should not use it in your writing.

✗ *There are less accidents where you have street lighting.*

✓ *There are **fewer** accidents where you have street lighting.*

Determiners

❖ **Activity 7 Amounts (1)**
Fill in the gaps using the determiners below.

an   all   every   the   a few   no   little   the   a

1 Every chemical element is composed of atoms, and at _____ nucleus, at the heart of _____ atom, is the proton, without which _____ matter could exist. Protons are the key to _____ creation.

2 I seemed to hear _____ low whistle, and _____ moments later a clanging sound.

3 There can be _____ doubt that this tortoise is _____ aboriginal inhabitant of _____ Galapagos Islands.

Some determiners are also **pronouns**. To tell the difference, remember that determiners are used at the beginning of a noun group, while pronouns are used on their own.

*'Can you see **any** snowflakes?'* (determiner)
*'No, there aren't **any**.'* (pronoun)

You can use *of* after most of these determiners when you want to talk about an amount of a specific thing.

▹ We were determined to prove ***all of*** those people wrong.
▹ He worked with ***many of*** Britain's top comic actors.
▹ I have great confidence in ***both of*** them.

❖ **Activity 8 Amounts (2)**
There is a difference in meaning between the sentences in **one** of these two pairs. Which is it?

1 He spent ***most afternoons*** watching football.
   He spent ***most of the afternoon*** watching football.

2 ***Neither boy*** had a pilot's licence.
   Neither of the boys had a pilot's licence.

Prepositions

Prepositions are another class of little words that do very important work in the sentence. They are followed by a **noun group**. There are many types of preposition, all with different uses.

Types and uses of prepositions

Prepositions of place
These tell you **where** someone or something is, or where they are going. The most frequent are *in*, *to*, *on*, *at*, *by* and *from*.

⟩ There were blackbirds sitting **on** *the telegraph wires*.
⟩ His friends had gone away **to** *Egypt*.

Other prepositions of place are:

under	*behind*	*between*	*underneath*
beside	*into*	*near*	*off*
above	*below*	*towards*	*through*
out of	*on top of*	*in front of*	*away from*

⟩ Mrs Martin stood firmly **between** *him and the door*.
⟩ We sat **in front of** *Charlie's house* for hours.

 Standard and non-standard: In your writing, be careful to use the preposition correctly:

✓ *He flew **out of** the door in a rage.*

✗ *He flew out the door in a rage.*

Out the door is acceptable in American English.

Prepositions

❖ **Activity 9 Prepositions of place**

Rewrite the sentences using a preposition with the 'opposite' meaning.

Example:

The car park had four levels **above** ground.

The car park had four levels **below** ground.

1   There were hundreds of people walking **towards** the main square.

2   She piled her books **underneath** her desk.

3   They jumped **out of** the train just as it began to move.

4   I found him sitting on a bench **behind** the restaurant.

5   He has just come back **to** our camp in the valley.

Prepositions of time

These tell you **when** something happens, or for **how long** it lasts. Some of them are the same as the very common place prepositions, but used with different nouns.

> ▸ I'm meeting him **on** Sunday.
> ▸ The train gets in **at** six fifteen.
> ▸ I haven't played chess **for** five years.

Other prepositions of time are *after*, *before*, *till*, *until*, *since* and *during*.

> ▸ Usually he slept **during** the daytime and went out only **after** dark.

Linking prepositions

Prepositions have many uses. For example, there are some **two-word** and **three-word prepositions** that you could find very useful for linking the parts of a sentence together.

because of	*except for*	*as well as*	*as for*
according to	*in spite of*	*thanks to*	*apart from*

> ▸ Marwan has lived in the West Bank all his life, **except for** *a brief spell in Canada.*
> ▸ Thurston missed a chunk of the season **because of** *a knee injury.*
> ▸ Wild celebrations broke out **in spite of** *the curfew.*

❖ **Activity 10 Linking prepositions**

Fill in the gaps using the prepositions below.

apart from   thanks to   as well as   as for   according to

1 West London missed Cole's wonder goal _____ a blackout.

2 There was nothing in the fridge _____ a bottle of champagne.

3 She had to wear blue hair extensions _____ a lot of jewellery.

4 _____ the BBC, a falling tree may have caused the accident.

5 _____ lunch, most days I brought my own food.

Prepositions

The most common preposition is *of*, which has hundreds of uses.

a packet of tea   *the meaning of life*   *the bottom of the sea*
the aim of the course   *a cry of pain*   *fond of his sister*

 Many prepositions are also **adverbs**. To tell the difference, remember that prepositions are followed by a **noun group**, while adverbs go together with **verbs**.

> *The blast knocked Dravic **off** <u>his feet</u>.* (preposition)
> *Suddenly the flash <u>went</u> **off**.* (adverb)

Conjunctions

There are two main kinds of conjunction, **co-ordinating conjunctions** and **subordinating conjunctions** – long names for little words.

Co-ordinating conjunctions

The main co-ordinating conjunctions are *and*, *but* and *or*. *And* is the most common – it is one of the most frequently used words in the English language.

CONJUNCTION

> ❖ **Activity 11 Discussion**
>   Discuss with a partner which words are as frequent as or more frequent than 'and' in English.

The work of co-ordinating conjunctions is to **link** parts of a sentence together.

▸ She gazed around frantically at the passengers hurrying *to **and** fro*. (words)
▸ She has *a new baby **and** a three-year-old*. (groups)
▸ She decided she *would go **and** visit* him. (chains)
▸ *The scheme may seem unfair **but** it works*. (clauses)

You can also use *yet* as a co-ordinating conjunction to mean the same as *but*, but it is much less common.

▸ The lush greenery looked alien **yet** oddly pleasant.

> **Our changing language:** Although conjunctions are a closed class, the word *plus* seems to be catching on as a 'new' co-ordinating conjunction, linking groups or clauses. It has more emphasis than *and*.
>
> > There's room for five adults **plus** plenty of luggage.
> > He can do anything Sam can do, **plus** he's younger and fitter.

❖ **Activity 12 Co-ordinating conjunctions**
Fill in the gaps using **and**, **but** or **or**.

1 I'm practising four _____ five hours every day.

2 He tried to contact his former colleagues, _____ they wouldn't talk to him.

3 She came home from the Olympics with two gold medals _____ a bronze.

4 Our high attic room was small _____ adequate.

5 She's getting little _____ no exercise.

6 I left home _____ went to live in New York.

For more information about linking clauses and sentences with co-ordinating conjunctions, see Part 5, page 145.

Subordinating conjunctions

There are a lot of subordinating conjunctions, but they too are a closed class. The most common ones are *as*, *if*, *when*, *because*, *although* and *while*.

The work of subordinating conjunctions is also to link together parts of the sentence. They usually link a **main clause** with a **subordinate clause**. (The subordinate clause is less important than the main clause.)

▸ He would lose everything *if* anyone found out what was going on.

▸ Otto visited you in hospital *while* you were still unconscious.

Note that subordinating conjunctions always come at the beginning of the clause that they introduce, so they can come either at the beginning or in the middle of the sentence.

❖ **Activity 13   Before you start**
Link the clauses using **because, while, when, if** or **although**, either at the beginning or in the middle, whichever sounds more natural.

1   Each face was different. They were all in some way familiar to me.

2   I understood my grandfather's feelings. He talked of his life in Africa.

3   Bert was cleaning out the dining room. He had discovered a pile of old yellowing maps.

4   He sought out Joanna. He expected her to protect him.

5   You miss another rehearsal. We will find someone else for the part.

Types and uses of subordinating conjunctions
There are different types of subordinating conjunction. These are the most important.

Time
Conjunctions: *when, whenever, after, before, since, till, until, once, while, as soon as*.

These conjunctions link events or situations together in a **sequence** of some sort.

▸ *When* I got to Athens I had to try and find the hospital. Then *once* I'd found the hospital, I had to try to find Sarah.

▸ She always wiped her hands on her jeans *after* she ate.

Conjunctions

 After, before, since, till and *until* are also **prepositions**. To tell the difference, remember that conjunctions are followed by a **clause**, while prepositions are followed by a **noun group**.

> I stared at him **until** <u>he looked away</u>. (conjunction)
> They sat in the cold empty room **until** <u>the morning</u>. (preposition)

Place

Conjunctions: *where, wherever*.

> ▸ **Wherever** he goes, he attracts a crowd.

Conditions

Conjunctions: *if, unless, as long as, so long as*.

These begin clauses that tell you about a possible action or situation, while the rest of the sentence tells you about the consequences of this. *Unless* is **negative** – it means 'if not'.

> ▸ **If** bees stay at home, rain will soon come. (old saying)
> ▸ We will vote against the proposal **unless** changes are made.

Reason

Conjunctions: *because, since, as, in case*.

These begin clauses that tell you why something happens or why a situation exists.

> ▸ He can't practise for a while, **as** he can't put any weight on his knee.
> ▸ I keep my valuables in the cellar, **in case** the house burns down.

Did you know...? In poetry and literature, *for* was often used to mean *because*, but it is old-fashioned:

He was a rat, and she was a rat,
And down in one hole they did dwell,
...
So he ventured out, and he ventured out,
And I saw them go with pain;
But what befell them I never can tell,
For *they never came back again.*
(anon.)

There is a verb chain in this poem that is different from what we say today, as well as some old-fashioned words. Can you find all these?

Purpose

Conjunctions: *so that, to, in order to, so as to.*

These begin clauses that tell you about what someone aims to achieve.
  ▸ Japan argues that it needs to kill whales ***in order to*** study them.

Result

Conjunctions: *so, so that.*
  ▸ My shoes had started to leak, ***so (that)*** my socks were soon uncomfortably wet.

Contrast

Conjunctions: *though, although, whereas, while, whilst.*

These begin clauses that make a contrast of some kind between ideas or situations. When one of the situations is surprising in some way, you can use *even though*.
  ▸ Maisie thought I was blaming her, ***although*** that was not true.
  ▸ Our team gave a tremendous performance, ***even though*** we were hit by injury and illness.
  ▸ My grandmother was a well-organized housewife, ***whereas*** my mother loathed any domestic activity.

Conjunctions

❖ **Activity 14 Subordinating conjunctions**
Fill in the gaps using the conjunctions below.

even though   as soon as   whenever   in case   if

1 He checked the papers through again _____ he'd missed something.

2 _____ she had stuck to the plan, she'd have been safely at the snake pit by now.

3 Ming wanted to walk home, _____ he knew it would take over an hour.

4 _____ everyone was ready, Bret coughed and began to speak.

5 A brilliant blue digital display lights up _____ a call is made or received.

For more information about linking clauses and sentences with subordinating conjunctions, see Part 5, page 148.

Forming words and phrases

Word families

Word families are **groups of words** that are related in some way. There are two main kinds of word family:

- **Form-based families**, where words have basically the same **stem** as each other (like *friend*, *friendless*, *friendly*, un*friendly*, *friendliness*, *friendship* and be*friend*).
- **Meaning-based families**, where there is no common stem but the words are related in meaning (like **happy**, **joyful**, **glad** and **sad**).

Form-based families

Look at these words:
- *appear*, **dis**appear, **re**appear
- *appearance*, **dis**appearance, **re**appearance

These words are clearly related to each other. The **stem** is *appear*, which is a **verb**. But you can change its form and meaning by adding different letters to it.

- If you add *dis*- at the beginning you get *disappear*, a verb with the **opposite** meaning.
- If you add *re*- at the beginning you get *reappear*, a verb that means *appear* **again**.
- If you add *-ance* at the end of any of these three words, you get a **noun** referring to the action of the verb.

The letters you add to the beginning are called **prefixes**, and the letters you add to the end are called **suffixes**.

When you add a **prefix**, the new word is usually of the **same** word class, but its meaning has changed – it might be an opposite, like *happy* → *unhappy*. When you add a **suffix**, the new word is usually of a **different** word class, for example a verb becomes a noun, as in *appear* → *appearance*, or a noun becomes an adjective, as in *sorrow* → *sorrowful*.

Now look at these:
- *act*, **re**act

Word families

> *action,* **re**action
> *actor,* **re**actor

Here the **stem** is *act*, again a verb.

- The prefix *re-* gives you *react*, a verb meaning 'to respond to something by behaving in a particular way', so this *re-* is a bit different from the one in *reappear*.
- The suffix *-ion* gives you *action* and *reaction*, nouns referring to an action. (Here one of them just happens to be *action* itself.)
- The suffix *-or* you gives you *actor*, meaning 'a **person** who acts' – it tells you someone's job or hobby. Another common suffix for this is *-er*, as in *singer* and *photographer*.

❖ **Activity 1 Before you start**
Fill in the gaps by adding a suitable prefix or suffix from the list below.

il- -al im- inter- -ance -ment un- dis-

1 It is wanting luxuries you can't afford that makes you __happy and __contented.

2 The winners of the competition then take part in nation__ and __national events.

3 At his trial the captain claimed that the war was __legal and __moral.

4 The perform__ ended in chaos, much to the amuse__ of the crowd.

We shall now look at

- prefixes and suffixes in more detail
- families that contain words that look the same but are used differently.

Changing form and meaning: prefixes

You add a **prefix** to the **beginning** of a word. Here is a list of some common prefixes. Many of them come from **Latin** or **Greek**, so the meanings of some of them may not be obvious to you.

Verbs

re-	*re*consider, *re*freeze, *re*open, *re-read*	(do again)
dis-	*dis*agree, *dis*approve, *dis*obey, *dis*like	(do the opposite)
mis-	*mis*behave, *mis*judge, *mis*manage	(do badly)
un-	*un*do, *un*pack, *un*dress, *un*wrap	(reverse an action)

Nouns

dis-	*dis*approval, *dis*belief, *dis*like	(negative feeling etc)
in-	*in*efficiency, *in*security, *in*ability	(lack of *efficiency* etc)
ex-	*ex*-husband, *ex*-prime minister	(former role/job)

Adjectives

un-	*un*kind, *un*certain, *un*tidy, *un*able	(not *kind* etc)
in-	*in*formal, *in*dependent, *in*secure	(not *formal* etc)
im-	*im*patient, *im*mature, *im*possible	(not *patient* etc)
il-	*il*legal, *il*logical, *il*literate	(not *legal* etc)
anti-	*anti*-nuclear, *anti*-war, *anti*-racist	(against)
inter-	*inter*national, *inter*planetary	(between)

But note that there are no fixed rules about the meaning of prefixes.

Did you know...? **Opposites** are not always predictable. For example, the prefix *in-* is usually used to make the **opposite** meaning of an adjective. But the adjective *invaluable* means 'so valuable that you cannot put a price on it', so it is not the opposite of *valuable*.

*I had **invaluable** help from my family during my recovery.*

Word families

Also, you can't predict whether a particular prefix will give you the meaning you want. For example, something may be *easy*, but the opposite is not *uneasy* – it's *difficult*.

    ▸ This is an **easy** question.
    ✗ This is an uneasy question.
    ✓ This is a **difficult** question.
    ✓ I had an **uneasy** feeling.

> **Our changing language:** The adjective **in**flammable means 'catches fire easily' or 'is easily ignited'. This used to be written on nightwear labels, hairsprays etc, to warn people not to get too close to a fire with them.
>
> Some people thought **in**flammable means 'can't catch fire', or 'non-combustible', because they knew that the prefix in- is usually negative. So manufacturers changed their labels, and decided to use **flammable** as a warning instead.

You can sometimes add two different prefixes to a word to make opposites with different meanings, for example the nouns **dis**use and **mis**use.

    ▸ The road fell into **disuse** after the end of the decade.
    ▸ The farmer was found guilty of pesticide **misuse**.

 What is the opposite of *interested*? The adjective *interested* has two opposites, **un**interested and **dis**interested, as shown here:

*Mona claimed to be completely **un**interested in fashion.*
*It was a major research centre for **dis**interested scholarship.*

The difference in meaning is clear from the examples above – **dis**interested means 'not interested for personal gain' or 'impartial'. But more and more people now wrongly use **dis**interested with the same meaning as **un**interested, that is, 'bored' or simply 'not interested'.

    ✗ *Mona claimed to be completely disinterested in fashion.*

You should use these words correctly in your writing.

Word families

 Punctuation: Note that some prefixes are usually used with a hyphen.

*minister, **ex**-minister*
*democratic, **pro**-democratic*
*grown, **home**-grown*
*smoker, **non**-smoker*

Some prefixes may need a hyphen with some words but not others.

*build, **re**build   examine, **re**-examine*
*day, **mid**day   afternoon, **mid**-afternoon*

Sometimes you have a choice. So this is an area where there may be no 'right' punctuation!

*matter, **anti**matter, **anti**-matter*

❖ **Activity 2 Prefixes (1)**
Here are some more examples of prefixes (in **bold**). What do you think they mean in the words below?

1 The boats will sail round the island in an **anti**-clockwise direction.

2 She is a wealthy heiress and a Bollywood **mega**star.

3 Try to avoid food that is **over**cooked, **pre**prepared or **re**heated.

4 Two flights were cancelled, one domestic, one **trans**atlantic.

5 A number of hospital patients are suffering from **mal**nutrition.

Can you think of other words that have the same prefixes?

There is another group of prefixes that are very important, especially in science and mathematics. They are all to do with **numbers** or **measures**. They all come from Latin or Greek, and you need to know as many of them as possible. The main ones are:

bi-	***bi**cycle, **bi**plane, **bi**lateral, **bi**sect*	(two)
tri-	***tri**cycle, **tri**angle, **tri**lateral*	(three)
multi-	***multi**-coloured, **multi**-media, **multi**-storey*	(many)
semi-	***semi**-circle, **semi**-detached, **semi**-tone*	(half)

Word families

deci-	*deci*mal, *deci*bel, *deci*litre	(10/10th)
centi-	*centi*grade, *centi*pede, *centi*litre	(100/100th)
kilo-	*kilo*byte, *kilo*gram, *kilo*metre, *kilo*watt	(1000)
milli-	*milli*second, *milli*gram, *milli*metre, *milli*litre	(1000th)

> **Did you know…?** The prefix *milli-* usually means a thousandth part of something, so for example there are 1,000 *milli*metres in a metre. But the word *million* means not 1,000 but 1,000,000. This comes from Italian and originally just meant 'a large thousand'. And *billion*, *trillion* etc followed logically from there.

❖ **Activity 3 Prefixes (2)**

Using the list above, add a prefix to the words or syllables below to make words that would fit into the gaps. Then write them into the gaps.

    ____storey   ____metres   ____lingual   ____pede
             ____pede   ____metres

1 The surgeons had to join blood vessels of only two _____ in diameter.

2 Signs are written in Chinese and English, and the staff are all _____ .

3 The difference between a _____ and a _____ is the number of legs each has per segment.

4 This walrus was a huge animal, with tusks about 60 _____ long.

5 London's first _____ car park was built in 1937.

❖ **Activity 4 Prefixes – general knowledge**
If you do not know the answers to these questions, discuss them
with a partner and try to find out.

1 A **kilobyte** is 1024 bytes (roughly 1000). How big are **megabytes**
   and **gigabytes** in relation to a kilobyte?

2 What exactly does the prefix **nano-** mean in words like
   nanotechnology, **nano**metre, **nano**second and **nano**particle?

Our changing language: The Internet is introducing new prefixes
into the language. One is *cyber*.

*cyber*space   **cyber**-*bullying*   **cyber**-*crime*   **cyber**café

  Schools must protect children from **cyber-bullying** *and other*
  online threats.

Do you know any more words beginning with *cyber-*?

Changing form and meaning: suffixes

You add a **suffix** to the **end** of a word. Note that the **spelling** of a word
often changes a bit when you add a suffix.

*adore, ador**able***   *beau**ty**, beaut**iful***
*possibl**e**, possib**ility***   *organiz**e**, organiz**ation***
*expla**in**, explan**ation***   *conclu**de**, conclu**sion***

These are some of the common suffixes.

You use these suffixes to form **nouns** from verbs or other nouns:

-ion	inform**ation**, protect**ion**, connect**ion**, exhibit**ion**, decis**ion**
-ance	assist**ance**, perform**ance**, attend**ance**, guid**ance**, disturb**ance**
-ence	occur**rence**, exist**ence**, depend**ence**, resid**ence**, interfer**ence**
-ment	amaze**ment**, employ**ment**, enjoy**ment**, punish**ment**
-ism	vandal**ism**, terror**ism**, capital**ism**, femin**ism**, hero**ism**

You use these suffixes to form nouns referring to people and what they do:

Word families

-er *baker, driver, employer, photographer, teacher, writer*
-or *narrator, creator, instructor, sailor, visitor, collector*
-ist *terrorist, arsonist, capitalist, feminist, tourist, extremist*

 But you can't predict … When you add *-or* to *react*, you get *reactor* (as in *nuclear reactor*) which is different – it is a machine, not a person.

This shows you again that although there are some regular meanings that prefixes and suffixes have, there are no fixed **rules** as there are in grammar.

> **Did you know…?** When a word has a particular kind of suffix, this does not always mean that the suffix is attached to a word that exists by itself.
>
> So you use *sing*, *singer* and *act*, *actor*, but there is no simple verb related to *tailor*, *author* or *doctor*.

❖ **Activity 5 Noun suffixes**
Add suffixes to make **nouns** from the verbs below. The suffix is the same in each pair, though you may have to change the spelling a little.

1 **educate**	**conclude**
2 **appear**	**insure**
3 **argue**	**achieve**
4 **prefer**	**interfere**
5 **farm** (person)	**paint** (person)

You use these suffixes to form **adjectives**:

-al *accidental, emotional, continental, regional, educational*
-able *acceptable, predictable, imaginable, advisable, bearable*
-ic *gymnastic, magnetic, heroic, enthusiastic, angelic*

-less use**less**, meaning**less**, end**less**, thought**less**, spot**less**

You use this suffix to form **adverbs**:

-ly immediate**ly**, clear**ly**, easi**ly**, soft**ly**, natural**ly**, normal**ly**

❖ **Activity 6 Adjective and adverb suffixes**

Add suffixes to make **adjectives** from the nouns and verbs below. Again, the suffix is the same in each pair.

1 **prefer**   **notice**

2 **idiot**   **photograph**

3 **logic**   **music**

4 **end**   **harm**

Make **adverbs** from these adjectives. You may have to change the spelling a little.

exact   **happy**

❖ **Activity 7 More suffixes**

Here are some more suffixes (in **bold**).

1 She appeared in a hand**ful** of movies in 1994.

2 Garnish the fish with a hand**ful** of chopped chives.

3 What is remark**able** about her letter is its pain**ful** honest**y**.

4 Her company voted her 'employ**ee** of the month'.

5 I didn't have an easy child**hood**.

6 Samir had a nightmar**ish** vision of his life slow**ly** collapsing.

7 He began appearing in small**ish** roles in a number of films.

8 Place the sausages in a flame**proof**, oven**proof** dish.

9 We try to eat foods that haven't been treated with pesti**cides**.

Word families

Discuss the following questions.

What do you think each suffix is being used to mean?

Does **handful** mean the same in **1** and **2**?

Does the suffix -**ish** mean the same in **6** and **7**?

Look at all the words with suffixes. Are they verbs, nouns or adjectives?

Can you think of other words that have the same suffixes?

❖ **Activity 8 The suffix '-style'**

The word **style** is being used more and more as a suffix, rather like '-ish'.

Example:

He has spent £800 per tooth to get a gleaming **Hollywood-style** smile.

Suggest one or more suitable beginnings from the list to fill in the gaps.

French   American   Mediterranean   family   Australian

1 The houses come complete with _____-**style** hot tubs and saunas.

2 Firefighters in Surrey battled hundreds of _____ -**style** bush fires.

3 Meals are served _____ -**style**, and everyone gets to know each other.

4 A _____ -**style** diet is rich in olive oil, whole grains, and vegetables.

5 A 'fat-free' _____-**style** salad dressing may have eight per cent sugar, plus stabilizers and colourings.

Note that the suffix **-ful** does not have double **l** at the end:

✓ hope**ful**	✗ hopefull
✓ spoon**ful**	✗ spoonfull

But **-less** keeps the double **ss**, showing you that English spelling can be very tricky.

✓ end**less**	✗ endles
✓ spot**less**	✗ spotles

Did you know…? There are some words that have a negative prefix or suffix, but there is no positive word – there is no 'opposite'.

You get **dis**gruntled, but have you met someone who gets gruntled?

People can be ruth**less**, but what is ruth?

People make **in**ane jokes, but have you ever heard one that is ane?

Changing meaning: families with the same forms

Sometimes you don't need to add a suffix to change a word to a different class, as there are hundreds of words that are the same or nearly the same across more than one class, especially **verbs** and **nouns**.

These are some of the most common words that are both verbs and nouns:

time	work	look	call	hand
place	start	run	help	change
question	move	order	pay	travel

▸ Can you **help** me? (verb)
▸ Can you give me some **help**? (noun)

Sometimes the **pronunciation** is different, for example use, house and produce.

Word families

❖ **Activity 9 Different sounds**
Say these sentences aloud:

1 Rates include the **use** of an indoor pool. (noun)
It's illegal to **use** a hand-held mobile while driving. (verb)

2 There's going to be demand for land to **produce** these crops. (verb)
Demand for organic **produce** is increasing faster than supply. (noun)

Some verbs and nouns are different in just one or two letters, for example:

verb	noun	verb	noun
li*ve*	li*fe*	belie*ve*	belie*f*
*a*ffect	*e*ffect	licen*se*	licen*ce*
practi*se*	practi*ce*	advi*se*	advi*ce*

▸ We want to **advise** young people against losing their family traditions. (verb)
▸ Children need love, help and **advice**, not TV advertising. (noun)
▸ After this tournament I'm going to **practise** as hard as I can for the next one. (verb)
▸ Change your clothes when you get back from football **practice**! (noun)

Variation: In British English, the spelling *practice* is used for the noun, and *practise* for the verb. Americans use **practice** as both a noun and a verb:

*He prefers to **practice** six days a week for ninety minutes, but sometimes misses a **practice**.*

If you live in Britain, you should use the British spelling in your writing.

Affect* or *effect*?** These words are often confused. Remember that ***affect is a verb, and ***effect*** is a noun.

> *Your early eating habits will **affect** you later in life.*
> *Research is being done into the long-term **effect** of TV on kids.*

❖ **Activity 10 'affect' or 'effect'?**
Fill in the gaps using a form of 'affect' or 'effect'.

1 Changes in sea temperature _____ penguins and seals in the Antarctic.

2 The biggest _____ of the floods is people's shattered lives.

3 The mercury in fish has harmful _____ on living organisms.

4 New technologies _____ almost everyone, whatever their age.

5 We need to know more about the causes and _____ of global warming.

6 All train services in the area _____ by the floods.

❖ **Activity 11 Verb or noun?**
Look at the words in **bold** and decide whether each is a verb or a noun.

1 There is an 18% **increase** in passenger travel to China each year.

2 Firefighters are still battling to **control** the flames.

3 The two would **practise** guitar together in Ron's apartment.

4 We hope to repeat yesterday's **result** in the FA cup final.

5 It was a large-scale **study** of food adverts aimed at children.

Which noun is **pronounced** differently from its related verb?

Which verb is **spelt** differently from its related noun?

Word families

More examples of form-based families

You can see that by using a combination of prefixes, suffixes and similar forms, you can take a basic stem and form a cluster of related words around it, all with different meanings.

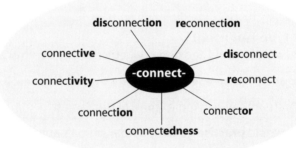

> **Our changing language:** 'Verbing' is not the only creative thing we do with word class. There is also 'nouning'. Note that ***disconnect*** (above) seems to have 'become' a noun as well as a verb, as in this example:
>
> *There seems to be a **disconnect** between the president and the public at large.*

This is another example of a form-based family. The stem, ***comfort***, is both a noun and a verb:

> ❖ **Activity 12 Form-based families**
> Make similar diagrams for the following stems. Try to find as many related words as you can.
>
> 1 **employ**   4 **exhaust**
>
> 2 **depend**   5 **collect**
>
> 3 **interest**   6 **mix**

Meaning-based families

This is the second main type of word family. In meaning-based families, the words have related **meanings**, although they have a completely different **form**.

Word families

❖ **Activity 13 Before you start**

Look at the groups of words below. What relationships do they have with each other? Do any of them mean the same? Are any of them related in a different way?

1 large, small

2 filthy, grimy, grubby

3 giraffe, goat, deer, horse, chimpanzee

4 sentence, paragraph, chapter, section, book

5 viewer, remote control, channel, programme

In the next sections you can learn about some ways in which words are related. The most typical groups or pairs of words are **synonyms** and **opposites**.

Synonyms

A lot of words are **synonyms**, that is, they mean almost the same as each other. But you have to be very careful when you choose a synonym. For example, these verbs all mean roughly the same:

complain   *grumble*   *moan*   *whine*   *whinge*

Of them all, *complain* is the most common and can be used in most situations. *Whinge* is the most informal.

▸ I shall **complain** to the highest authorities about our treatment.

▸ It's boring when your friends ***whinge*** all the time.

You couldn't use any of the other words in the first sentence above.

✗ I shall grumble / moan / whine / whinge to the highest authorities...

And you'd probably never use *whine* or *whinge* about yourself anyway, because they show irritation. So it is better to think of all these words as **near-synonyms** rather than true synonyms.

Another set of near-synonyms might be:

obese	*fat*	*buxom*	*stout*	*overweight*
ample	*plump*	*chubby*	*curvy*	

You can use all these to describe people, but only *curvy* is complimentary. No-one likes to be called *obese* or *fat* or even *chubby*. *Stout*, *buxom* and *plump* are rather old-fashioned, and *ample* is usually used for bits of your body – an *ample backside* or *ample hips*. *Overweight* is the most 'neutral'.

So again you have to choose your adjective carefully.

 ▸ Mounira had a ***plump***, friendly face.
 ⤳ She had an ***ample***, friendly face.
 ▸ A growing percentage of people are ***overweight*** or ***obese***.
 ⤳ A growing percentage of people are plump or chubby.

Synonyms also 'go together' with different words, for example:

 ▸ Whoever wins the final on Sunday will be handed a ***fat*** *cheque*.
 ▸ There were ***plump*** *pillows* and duvets in every bedroom.

The two adjectives above are not **interchangeable** – you don't often talk about a *plump cheque* or a *fat pillow*. The way words combine like this is called **collocation** (see pages 106–8).

So the point is that some words do mean roughly the same, but they don't **collocate** with the same other words. So first of all you can collect a group of synonyms, but then you need to look at the **differences** between them.

❖ **Activity 14 Near-synonyms**
   Fill in the gaps using the near-synonyms below. Discuss the reasons for your choices. Are there any words that are interchangeable?

   skinny   slender   lean   thin   slim   scrawny

   1 I lay on the mattress with only a _____ blanket over me.

   2 Choose _____ cuts of meat and trim off any fat.

   3 She poured wine into tall, _____ glasses.

   4 _____ chickens and ducks scrabbled in the dust for scraps.

   5 The jacket could be worn with a _____ black skirt.

   6 In the no-mercy world of fashion, _____ jeans are back.

Word families

You can use all the words in Activity 14 above to describe a person, and again, some are more complimentary and positive than others. The words in the next examples are not interchangeable – try!

▶ She's tall and fit and **slim**, with shiny streaked chestnut hair.
▶ Fred was a bit **scrawny** now in his old age, but he was as active as ever.

Opposites

Another important relationship between words is that some of them have the **opposite** meaning from each other. You have already seen how, in **form-based families** (see pages 79–93), prefixes like -*un* and -*in* give a word an opposite meaning. In meaning-based families, opposites have no stem in common.

Here are some pairs of opposites:

big, little	*hot, cold*	*fast, slow*
old, young	*fat, thin*	*hard, soft*

 Different meanings – different opposites: Some words have more than one opposite, with different meanings. *Old* here has two:

> *Very <u>young</u> and very **old** people are most at risk from heatstroke.*
> *The group will play a mixture of **old** and <u>new</u> songs.*

And *hot* here has two different opposites:

> *Add a few <u>mild</u> or **hot** chopped green chillies.*
> *<u>Cold</u> weather brings thoughts of **hot** soup.*

There are other relationships that are not really opposites, but relate to different **roles** people have in their lives:

buy, sell	*borrow, lend*	*teacher, student*

▶ She **borrowed** my black dress to wear at a party.
▶ I **lent** her a beautiful sari that my sister no longer wears.

Other relationships

Some words are related because they belong in the same **class** or **category**, for example:

mammal: mouse, dog, cat, sheep, goat, pig, cow, monkey, man
language: French, Russian, Arabic, Japanese, English, Gaelic
metal: aluminium, gold, silver, copper, uranium, tin, iron, lead

❖ **Activity 15 Categories – general knowledge**
  Think of as many words as possible that could complete the lists.

  1 **element**: hydrogen, zinc, _____ , _____ , _____

  2 **reptile**: crocodile, lizard, _____ , _____ , _____

  3 **shape**: circle, rectangle, _____ , _____ , _____

Some words are related because they are all **parts** of the same thing:

human body: hand, foot, leg, arm, face, eye, mouth, nose, ear
bicycle: wheels, gears, handlebars, pedals, chain, saddle, lights

❖ **Activity 16 Parts – general knowledge**
  Think of as many words as possible that could complete the lists.

  1 **car**: engine, accelerator, _____ , _____ , _____

  2 **tree**: trunk, twig, _____ , _____ , _____

  3 **computer**: monitor, hard drive, _____ , _____ , _____

Fields

Other words are related in a more general way. The following list is a
mixture of synonyms and other meaning relations. There are also different
word classes in the lists. The only thing the words have in common is that
they are about the same general **topic** (diet).

diet	carbohydrate	protein	fats	fibre
vitamins	minerals	vegetarian	vegan	consume
calorie	energy	nutrition	organic	GM crops

Word families

❖ **Activity 17 Word fields**

Technology is an area that has a big impact on the words we use. Think of as many words as you can that are connected with the topic of **the Internet**.

Examples: Google®, email, surf, chat-room, MySpace®...

Can you think of any other topics that have brought new words into English?

Compounds

Compounds are basically 'words' that consist of more than one word. They are formed by combining two (or three) words together and making a new bigger name for a person, thing, concept etc, or a new bigger adjective.

There are different ways of joining words together to make compounds and different ways of punctuating them.

Run-together compounds

Thousands of pairs of words have run together to become a compound, with no hyphen, and now we tend to forget that they used to be two words. They include the following **nouns**:

password	keyboard	gearbox	flowchart	newspaper
database	copyright	highlight	hardware	spreadsheet
firefly	netball	makeup	notebook	lifeboat

Many of the words above combine with other words as well, to make different compounds, for example *keystroke, newsagent, moonlight, keyword*.

❖ **Activity 18 Compound nouns**
Fill in the other half of the words in **bold** to make compounds. Use your own knowledge.

1 The full glare of the ____**light** again falls on Nicole Kidman.

2 The team developed specialized ____**ware** for analysing genetic data.

3 Australia's vast size makes it difficult to connect every home to a high-speed ____**work**.

4 Everything inside the computer is connected to a circuit board called the ____**board**.

5 The Herald has produced a glossy **wall**____ of Scottish birds.

6 Make sure you use a ____**band** connection, as dial-up takes longer.

Compounds

Some common nouns are used as the basis of a lot of single-word compound nouns:

head: *headache, headphones, headset, headline, headlamp, headway*

❖ **Activity 19   Compound nouns with 'sun'**

Fill in the gaps with a suitable word to combine with **sun**. Sometimes there is more than one possibility.

1   The cat was lying on the doorstep in a patch of **sun**_____ .

2   Are you expecting us to get through this jungle by **sun**_____ ?

3   She wore a chiffon top, silver shoes and wraparound **sun**_____ .

4   If you go to the beach, wear **sun**_____ , lots of it.

5   We watched the warm, pink **sun**_____ reflected in the skyscraper windows.

6   **Sun**_____ are planet-sized magnets created by the sun's inner magnetic dynamo. (If you don't know this, try to find out.)

Can you think of any more words that form compounds with **sun**?

Hyphenated and separate-word compounds

Other compounds are either **hyphenated** or remain two separate words. But there are no fixed rules for this as there usually are in grammar, and different people write compounds differently. Dictionary entries too may be different from one dictionary to another.

Some compounds are very often hyphenated. The next examples are **nouns** and **adjectives**:

dining-room	*cross-reference*	*stick-in the-mud*
free-range	*colour-blind*	*cutting-edge*
computer-literate	*late-night*	*accident-prone*

Again, many of the words above combine with other words as well, to make different compounds, for example *cross-breed*, *sitting-room*, *colour-coded*, *long-range*.

Many hyphenated compounds are formed using the *-ed* form of the verb. These compounds are usually **adjectives**.

home-made	*half-baked*	*mass-produced*
petroleum-based	*hand-held*	*ready-made*

> Nihaya has ***henna-coloured*** hair like dark copper.

Many compounds are formed using the *-ing* form of the verb. These are often nouns referring to sports and activities, or adjectives referring to characteristics.

spray-painting	*horse-riding*	*flower-arranging*
fun-loving	*good-looking*	*man-eating*

> She leaps fearlessly onto the backs of ***man-eating*** crocodiles.

Punctuation: You write:

a **four-year-old** girl	a **forty-four-year-old** woman
a **four-year-old**	She was **four years old**.

There is no hyphen when you use *years* instead of *year*.

Compounds

You write:

a **100-metre** race	the **third-largest** city
a **third-floor** flat	The flat was on the **third floor**.

A much larger number of compounds usually consist of two (or more) separate words. The next examples are all **nouns**:

food chain	bar chart	pulse rate	magnetic field
life cycle	human being	post office	middle class
full moon	blood pressure	public transport	light year
weather forecast	nuclear power station		

 A test of whether two words can be seen as a compound is whether you can put anything in between. In a true compound, like say *pulse rate*, you could not put anything between *pulse* and *rate*.

Note that a compound may not mean the same as its two words taken separately. For example, your **nervous system** is not 'nervous' in the way you normally use the word.

Spelling variations

There are many words that are used in all three versions: run-together, hyphenated, or separated.

air freight, air-freight, airfreight   *ice sheet, ice-sheet, icesheet*

▶ The Antarctic **ice sheets** / **ice-sheets** / **icesheets** are thawing at a great rate.

 Punctuation: This is good news for you. When you use some compounds, you can often be fairly free in your punctuation, and use a hyphen or not, as you choose. No-one is going to say you are wrong!

The reason punctuation varies is that **compounding** or **compound forming** is an ongoing process. As society, science and technology develop, new compounds emerge. As time goes on, the form of a compound becomes more fixed – it may eventually become a single word.

Some common words can be used to form a lot of compounds, run-together, hyphenated and separated:

fire: fireball, firework, fire-fighter, fire-eater, fire engine, fire escape

❖ **Activity 20 Compounds with 'free'**
Fill in the gaps with a suitable noun or adjective to combine with **free**, using the **form** (run-together, hyphenated or separated) that looks most natural.

1 They keep more than 400 **free** _____ hens up there in the hills.

2 It will then dive 2400m, the **free** _____ allowing passengers to experience zero gravity for around 25 seconds.

3 She won the 100m **free** _____ and came third in the butterfly.

4 Chelsea were awarded a **free** _____ in the 18th minute.

5 **Free** _____ is software that you can use without paying anything.

❖ **Activity 21 Vocabulary knowledge**
Fill in the other half of the words in **bold** to make compounds, using the form that seems most natural. Use your own knowledge.

1 Celeste taught him **sign** _____ and later **lip** _____ .

2 If you go back to the **home** _____ , you'll find links to all our online services.

3 He needs to show that he can do more than provide a neat _____ **bite** for TV.

4 The hot weather meant increased pollution in _____ **centres**.

5 I thought it was a joke, so I was waiting for the _____ **line**.

Compounds

Some newer compound nouns

Many compounds are becoming more and more frequent. For example, the way of measuring *body mass index* was invented in the nineteenth century, but the common use of the compound noun is recent. Statistics show that it was used 14 times more often in 2007 than in 1993.

  ▶ Madrid fashion week banned models with a **body mass index** (BMI) of less than 18.

  ▶ One in five British women is clinically obese, with a **body mass index** of 30 or more.

Other compounds that are rapidly becoming far more common than before are:

carbon footprint	*work-life balance*	*air miles*
global warming	*hen night*	*blogosphere*
congestion charge	*the glass ceiling*	*speed dating*
health tourism	*stem cell research*	*human genome*

In a lot of these cases, it is the activity itself that is new – older generations didn't have *hen nights* in the way women do today; they didn't grow up knowing about the threat of *global warming*; and many women didn't go out to work, so they had no problem with their *work-life balance*.

❖ **Activity 22 Newer compound nouns**

Make four compound nouns from the **eight** nouns in the list below. Then use them to fill in the gaps.

> **potato   gases   plasma   couch   change   screen climate   greenhouse**

1 A _____ _____ in one corner was showing a football match.

2 _____ _____ will inevitably increase the risk of flooding.

3 I was a _____ _____ before I joined the cricket team.

4 Carbon and methane are both _____ _____ .

One quite new change is that the word -*speak* is becoming attached to more and more nouns to make compounds – in fact, you can add it to a huge range of words:
business-speak, doctorspeak, double-speak, geek-speak, newspeak, tech-speak, teen-speak, text-speak, leetspeak.

▸ New Zealand's high school students will be able to use ***text-speak*** in national exams this year. Wud ur tchr hv let u?

Did you know...? The forming of new compounds is happening all the time. But there is also an opposite process going on – the **loss** of compounds. Some 'lost' compounds are:

mobile phone ➔ ***mobile***
remote control ➔ ***remote***
weblog (web log) ➔ ***blog***
microwave oven ➔ ***microwave***

Collocation and phrases

The other very important way in which words combine together is that you use lots of different **phrases**. You do not build up your sentences word by word – that would take far too long. Instead you use groups of words that naturally 'go together' with different variations. We say that these words **collocate** – they 'keep each other's company', although they are not compounds.

A lot of common verbs 'go with' particular nouns. For example, you *have a shower* (in America you *take a shower* though) and you *make, take,* or *come to* a decision.

❖ **Activity 23 Collocation**

Think of one or more verbs that 'go with' the nouns in **bold**, and use them to fill in the gaps.

1 So he had to _____ a **choice** in the end.

2 They have not yet _____ us a **reason** for the delay.

3 He's _____ some very rude **comments** about different people.

4 We're going to _____ a **break** now – all of you be back in 15 minutes!

5 I told George that I can't _____ the **point** of arguing about it.

6 Are they seriously trying to _____ a peaceful **solution** to the dispute?

7 His plan to _____ the **meeting** on Monday fell through.

8 _____ a **look** at this map.

9 Six thousand viewers complained that the programme _____ a bad **example** to children.

10 They have _____ no **link** between him and any terrorist organization.

Some collocations are fairly fixed. These all happen to be noun groups:

a low profile *an unknown quantity* *a heart of gold*
a waste of space *business as usual* *the 'war on terror'*
one of the lads *a bundle of nerves* *a can of worms*
flavour of the month *a grey area* *a change of heart*

These are all phrases based on verbs:

read between the lines *make the right noises* *go ballistic*
swallow your pride *rock the boat* *have cold feet*

❖ **Activity 24 Well-known phrases (1)**
Fill in the gaps with one or more words, using your own instincts about collocation and phrases.

1 I would be happy **beyond my** _____ **dreams** if I could buy a small house for my family.

2 The best doctors, the best nurses, want to work in a hospital that's **on the** _____ **edge** of medical research.

3 Calm down! Losing your mobile is not **a matter of** _____!

 Although we use these 'pre-fabricated' phrases all the time, there are many phrases that people overuse, and these tend to make your speech or writing sound unoriginal and boring. These are called *clichés* (pronounced *kleeshays*).

❓ *I have to agree it all went pear-shaped, but at the end of the day we have to put it behind us and move on.*

Many words are used in a huge number of phrases. Look at some of the phrases that contain the word *head*.

▹ I discovered that you had to ***have a good head for*** business, too.
▹ I've absolutely ***no head for heights***.
▹ She ***laughed her head off*** when I broke the bed.
▹ I ***couldn't make head nor tail of*** the keyboard control combos.
▹ Will you just listen without ***biting my head off***?
▹ When I was alone there, I ***went off my head*** from boredom.

Collocation and phrases

And there are many more. Note that there is a lot of variation in the use of the phrases – for example, the first one could have been *for figures, for facts* and so on, and you can leave out *good*.

❖ **Activity 25 Well-known phrases (2)**
What is the missing word in these groups of phrases?

1 She saw, in her mind's _____ , all those peculiar creatures.
   Natalia caught my _____ and smiled in encouragement.
   Vivek said he'd keep an _____ on the children for me.

2 Alan played well and gave it his best _____ .
   I didn't need telling twice. I was off like a _____ .
   I moved back home, very glad to be _____ of the hotel at last.

3 Mohan has too much _____ on his hands. He should get a job.
   Nassima had a movie career, but she never hit the big _____ .

Did you know…? Writers and poets often use unusual collocations to achieve a particular effect, or to make the reader think about something in a fresh and different way.

For example, the writer Vladimir Nabokov speaks of:
 his simple, functional nose *velvet eyebrows*
 the angelic sky   *pale, spellbound buildings*

And from Dylan Thomas:
 the sloeblack, slow, black, crowblack, fishingboat-bobbing sea
 in her iceberg-white, holily laundered crinoline nightgown, under
 virtuous polar sheets

Colours are another area where writers can be creative in their description by using unfamiliar collocations.
 the dishonest nursery blue of the sky
 the helplessly black garden

None of these are 'normal' collocations, but if you read them in context they are very effective, and add to the strong impact of the writer's narrative style.

From word to clause

Part 4

Groups and chains

Nouns combine with other words to form **noun groups**. Adjectives combine with other words to form **adjective groups**. Verbs combine with one or more **auxiliaries** to form **verb chains**.

Noun groups

Nouns can combine with **determiners**, **adjectives**, and other **nouns** to make noun groups. They can also be followed by a **prepositional phrase**, which is a preposition followed by another noun group.

The most important noun in the group is known as the **head** of the group.

Here are just a few examples of noun groups. There are many other combinations.

determiner + **noun**

the **theory**	my **opinion**	this **fact**
both **ways**	most **women**	plenty of **people**

adjective + **noun**

poisonous **snakes**	absolute **power**	huge **distances**
calming **music**	good **vocalists**	Hawaiian **music**

determiner + adjective + **noun**

a difficult **journey**	this brilliant **song**	my favourite **music**
a free **festival**	some terrible **mistakes**	no strong **feelings**

adjective + adjective + **noun**

thick grey **clouds**	short curly **hair**	shiny new **fabrics**
warm, shallow **seas**	loud, high **notes**	simple, catchy **songs**

noun + **noun**

plant **fibres**	leather **shoes**	raspberry **ice-cream**
steam **power**	cave **paintings**	daytime **television**

determiner + **noun** + prepositional phrase

the **surface** of the planet	some **facts** about the origins of life

Groups and chains

❖ **Activity 1   Noun groups**

Underline all the noun groups in these two parts of poems. Try to decide on the word class of the words in each noun group.

The Owl and the Pussy-Cat went to sea
In a beautiful pea-green boat,
They took some honey and plenty of money,
Wrapped up in a five-pound note.
The Owl looked up to the stars above,
And sang to a small guitar ...
(Edward Lear)

How doth the little crocodile
Improve his shining tail;
And pour the waters of the Nile
On every golden scale!

How cheerfully he seems to grin,
How neatly spreads his claws,
And welcomes little fishes in,
With gently smiling jaws!
(Lewis Carroll)

 In your writing, try to **expand** the central noun of a group by adding determiners, adjectives, nouns and prepositional phrases. It will make your writing more interesting. Notice how writers do this and the positive effect it has on a text.

She lived in ***a cottage in west Wales.***
She lived in ***a little old tumbledown cottage in the wilds of west Wales.***

A noun can be followed by a prepositional phrase to make a noun group. Note that some nouns are followed by a particular preposition.

▸ She thought that Susan was ***a bad influence*** *on* her brother.
▸ ***Safe protection*** *from* mosquito bites is particularly important.

❖ **Activity 2 Expanding noun groups**
The noun groups in these sentences consist only of a noun and a determiner. Expand them using **all** the words and phrases below.

> **very active   alleged   in the debate   blue   to us**
> **beautiful   against him   great   of water   shocking**

1 She assured him that he would play **a role**.

2 The support of family and friends at this time is **a comfort**.

3 **The charges** were dropped and he was free.

4 The unnecessary use of sprinklers is **a waste**.

5 His mother gave me **some glasses** as a present.

Try to think of other adjectives and prepositional phrases that you could use to add detail to the noun groups in these sentences.

Linking noun groups

Noun groups can be linked together to add information and detail.

You can put one noun group after another when the second one **defines** the first in some way, giving a name or a description. You usually put a comma after the first noun group.

> ... the famous vampire story, Bram Stoker's Dracula ...
> ... the waiter, a brightly-dressed character ...
> ... our closest living relative, the chimpanzee ...

❖ **Activity 3 Linking noun groups – definitions**
Using your general knowledge, match the two noun groups.

1 a giant fungus,	**a** the world's tallest trees
2 the blue whale,	**b** the world's largest land animal
3 the European hedgehog,	**c** the world's largest animal
4 Californian redwoods,	**d** the world's sleepiest mammal

Groups and chains

5 the African elephant,　　**e** the world's largest known organism

You can also link noun groups together using *and* (or *or*). You can cut down the second noun group by omitting (leaving out) some of the words.

› This book contains ***some intriguing questions*** and ***answers***.
› They're now offering ***electronic books*** and ***newspapers***.

The noun groups above 'share' a determiner and an adjective, or just an adjective. You don't need to say *some intriguing questions* and *some intriguing answers*, because it should still be clear what you mean. This is called **ellipsis**.

❖ **Activity 4 Linking noun groups – omitting words**
Which words could you cut out of the linked noun groups to make the sentence sound more natural?

1 The support vehicle was carrying **our new sleeping bags, our new tents and our new climbing gear**.

2 Rich visitors are shopping aggressively for **luxury bags, luxury watches and luxury designer clothes**.

You can put several noun groups together to make short lists. You usually put the **conjunction** *and* (or *or*) before the last noun group.

› We are planning to build ***sports facilities***, ***a large pool*** and ***a new music arena***.
› Children are allowed ***no iPods***, ***laptop computers***, ***video games*** or ***DVDs***.

> **Did you know...?** In literature and especially poetry, writers often put *and* between each noun group. This gives rhythm to a sentence.
>
> *You can have **a wonky nose** and **a crooked mouth** and **a double chin** and **stick-out teeth**, but if you have good thoughts they will shine out of your face like sunbeams...*

Some strings of noun groups can be quite long:

> They love **their overseas holidays**, **their villas in France**, **their second homes**, **their huge plasma televisions** and **their big gas-guzzling cars** …

 Punctuation: When you have a string of noun groups like this, you don't need a comma between the word 'and' *and* the last noun group. But sometimes it is better to put one, if that makes the meaning clearer.

*He was wearing **a well-fitting white sweater**, **frayed jeans**, and **a baseball cap over his eyes**.*

In American English, by the way, most people always put a comma before the *and*.

Adjective groups

Adjectives can combine with **adverbs** and **prepositional phrases** to make adjective groups. The adjective is the **head** of the adjective group.

Adverb + adjective

You can use a lot of different **degree adverbs** before some adjectives.

You can use some of them, such as *completely*, *absolutely* and *utterly* to **emphasize** your description of someone or something.

> Maybe their statistics are not **totally accurate**.
> His children are **utterly adorable**.
> It's hard work, but my brother is **perfectly capable**.

You can also use some degree adverbs before an adjective to show **how much** of a quality is present.

▸ Where I live, the rents are **fairly cheap**.

▸ Waking up feeling tired after a long sleep is **quite common**.

▸ I know my mum's been **extremely busy**.

❖ **Activity 5 Adjective groups with adverbs**

Fill in the gaps using the adverbs below to make adjective groups. There may be more than one possibility but some sound better.

> **perfectly   virtually   rather   completely
> slightly   remarkably**

1 The way football is played in Italy and England is _____ **different**.

2 I must say I found her behaviour _____ **odd**.

3 I'll be _____ **happy** if we get as far as the third round.

4 In spite of the pain, he was feeling _____ **calm**.

5 Juggling with six balls at the same time is _____ **difficult**.

6 My mother had a coat like that – it was _____ **identical**.

Adjective + prepositional phrase

You can also expand an adjective by adding a **prepositional phrase** (a preposition followed by a noun group).

> ▸ Birmingham is **famous as** the home of the industrial revolution.
> ▸ The workshop is **suitable for** all children over the age of ten.

Some adjectives are followed by particular prepositions.

ready for	**fond** of	**distant** from	**responsible** for
aware of	**keen** on	**interested** in	**similar** to
suitable for	**angry** with	**involved** in	**famous** for / as

❖ **Activity 6 Adjective + preposition**
Fill in the gaps with the most suitable preposition.

1 Most local people are **dependent** _____ **agriculture** for survival.

2 If you are **allergic** _____ **dairy products**, you won't be able to eat yoghurt.

3 As long as the children are **honest** _____ **me**, that's all I care about.

4 Some parents are not **good** _____ **discussing sex education**.

5 She tries to keep her work **separate** _____ **her family life**.

 Different from or *different to*? *Different from* is much more frequent in British English than *different to*, which is more common in American. Both are acceptable, but teachers usually prefer *from*.

> *She was somehow **different from** the woman he remembered.*
> *International football is **different to** club football.*

Americans often say *different than*, but teachers in Britain would probably consider that wrong.

> *He was **different than** a lot of the prisoners.*

You can link adjective groups together in the same way as noun groups, with commas or conjunctions such as *and*.

▸ another *very cold*, *horribly wet*, *dreadfully windy* day
▸ For his size, he is *extremely strong* and *very aggressive*.
▸ Maisie is *really charming* and *exceptionally clever*.

Verb chains
Verbs combine with auxiliaries to make **verb chains**.

Here are some examples of verb chains.

▸ Maliyah *doesn't like* chicken nuggets.
▸ We*'re leaving* by ship because the airport *is closed*.

‣ I **have finished** the draft of my report.
‣ By that time the war **had begun**.
‣ Overall we **have been playing** well this season.
‣ I **could stay** here for ever.

Verb + 'to'-infinitive or '-ing'

Sometimes you link two verb chains together. The second chain is a **to-infinitive** or **-ing** form.

These common verbs are often followed by a *to*-infinitive:

want	*refuse*	*continue*	*begin*	*expect*	*hope*
try	*manage*	*afford*	*fail*	*promise*	*decide*

In the next examples, the first verb chain is in **bold** and the second is underlined.

‣ When you are a player, you **don't want** to miss a game.
‣ He **has refused** to admit to any responsibility for the accident.
‣ A lot of people **decided** to escape from the mud and go home.

These common verbs are often followed by the *-ing* form of another verb:

like	*finish*	*enjoy*	*hate*	*love*	*imagine*
forget	*involve*	*suggest*	*consider*	*admit*	*risk*

‣ Fusion **involves** squeezing the nuclei of two atoms together.
‣ If you pay the agency in advance, you **may risk** losing your money.

verb chains

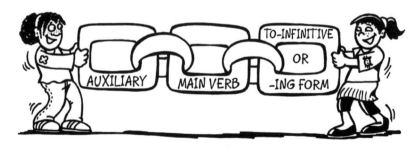

AUXILIARY MAIN VERB TO-INFINITIVE OR -ING FORM

❖ **Activity 7 Verb +** *to*-**infinitive or** *-ing*?
Fill in the gaps to make linked verb chains, using the correct form of the verb in brackets.

1 He **suggested** _____ (explore) some out-of-the-way places in California.

2 Firefighters **have managed** _____ (control) a blaze in south London.

3 We **are hoping** _____ (hear) his side of the story soon.

4 I **couldn't imagine** _____ (spend) the night in a haunted house.

5 We **couldn't afford** _____ (feed) ourselves properly back then.

Clauses

A **clause** is basically a group of words that contains a verb, and expresses an action, event or situation. It usually contains a subject and a verb. This should be the definition you work with.

A **sentence**, on the other hand, is just a stretch of language that begins with a capital letter and ends in a full stop.

A sentence can consist of one clause, two clauses, or more, as the next examples show.

1 Beavers erect sturdy dams in streams.

1 One beaver dam in the USA is 700 metres long **2** and can bear the weight of a horse.

1 When building a dam, **2** a beaver selects exactly the right tree, **3** then gnaws through it with its sharp incisors.

❖ **Activity 8 Before you start**
Decide how many clauses there are in these sentences, and number them.

1 The condition is highly infectious and passes very easily within families.

2 They tested the virus to see if it was infectious.

3 Called nanotube water, these molecules contain two hydrogen atoms and one oxygen atom but do not turn into ice.

The structure of clauses

As we said, a clause usually contains a verb. A typical simple clause contains a **subject**, a **verb**, and an **object**.

The **subject** (**S**) of a clause is often the 'doer' of an action, or is in some way responsible for what happens.

The **verb** (**V**) tells you what someone is doing, what is happening, or what the situation is. The **object** (**O**) is the person or thing that the action is 'done to' or that is affected by it in some way.

The subject and object are usually **noun groups** or **pronouns**.

She	*was defending*	*her daughter.*
S	**V**	**O**
Her daughter	*had married*	*an Australian.*
S	**V**	**O**
Christopher Wren	*designed*	*St Paul's Cathedral.*
S	**V**	**O**

Some verbs (called **intransitive** verbs) never have objects, and some can be used with or without one. So a sentence may contain just a subject and a verb.

My mother	*was complaining.*
S	**V**
All the kids	*laughed.*
S	**V**
Windows®	*is shutting down.*
S	**V**
The battle	*was won.*
S	**V**
The meal	*has been prepared.*
S	**V**

Instead of an object, some clauses have a **complement**. The job of a complement is to describe or identify the subject.

The complement comes after a **link verb** like *be*, *seem* and *appear*, though *be* (*is*, *was*, *were* etc) is by far the most common.

The complement is usually a **noun group** or **pronoun**, or an **adjective group**.

Alice	*is*	*a nice woman.*
S	V	C
Slugs	*are*	*disgusting.*
S	V	C
The idea	*seems*	*relatively simple.*
S	V	C

It and *there* are often the subjects of a clause. They are often called **empty subjects**, as they don't mean much in themselves.

It	*was*	*a dark and stormy night.*
S	V	C
There	*is*	*no magic formula.*
S	V	C

The simplest clause of all contains only a verb or verb chain – an **imperative**.

Fetch!
V
Don't shoot!
V

❖ **Activity 9 The structure of clauses**
Fill in the gaps with a suitable subject, object or complement from the noun and adjective groups below.

> **lack of oxygen   diamonds   respiration**
> **less oxygen   bacteria and viruses   more infectious**

1 The high altitude atmosphere contains _____ .

2 Is bird flu becoming _____ ?

3 _____ causes severe damage to the brain.

4 Doctors were monitoring his heart rate and _____ .

5 _____ are a natural form of pure carbon.

6 _____ can weaken your immune system.

Can you note which part of each clause is a subject (**S**), verb (**V**), object (**O**) or complement (**C**)?

> **Punctuation:** Note that you should not put a comma after the subject. This is a very common mistake.
>
> ✗ *Children who live in the city, sometimes don't know where their food comes from.*

All the clauses above are quite simple, but they lack any detail about **place**, **time**, **manner** or any other circumstances. To add these details, you use one or more **adverbials (A)**.

She	speaks	Arabic	fluently.
S	**V**	**O**	**A**

Adverbials in a clause are usually **adverbs** or **prepositional phrases**. These ones are adverbs:

▸ I understand you ***perfectly***.
▸ They waited ***anxiously***.
▸ People ***sometimes*** forget things.
▸ I'll find out ***somehow***.
▸ ***Soon*** it was time to leave.
▸ ***Physically***, I'm in good shape.

Clauses

These adverbials are prepositional phrases:

> *After this mission*, we will know the composition of Martian dust.
> Cave dwellers wore skins *for warmth*.
> *In dry weather*, pine cones dry up and open out.

The next examples have more than one adverbial.

> She sang *beautifully* *in a clear high voice*.
> The news wasn't all bad *for France's cyclists* *at the weekend*.
> We're meeting him *on Tuesday* *in the park*.

❖ **Activity 10 Adverbials**
Fill in the gaps using the adverbials below. They all refer to **time** in some way.

**immediately   for five minutes   during daylight
in twelve hours   by the 11th century   in the late 1800s**

1 The flu virus can invade one million nose and throat cells
   _____ .

2 Brown the dish under the grill _____ , then serve
   _____ .

3 Plants carry out photosynthesis _____ .

4 _____ , the French chemist Louis Pasteur realized that
   disease was carried by microscopic germs.

5 _____ , the Chinese were using movable type for
   printing.

There are three other adverbials in the sentences above. Can you find them? They are all prepositional phrases.

Types of clause: statement, question and imperative
Every finite clause is either a **statement**, a **question**, or an **imperative** (a command).

Statements

Statements are clauses that give information or state opinions.

The verb can be either **positive** or **negative**.
 ▸ Viruses *can produce* toxins that damage your cells. (positive)
 ▸ I *can't believe* the strength of some of those storms. (negative)

Questions

Questions are of two main kinds.

Sometimes you just want someone to say *yes* or *no* in reply to your question.

In **yes/no questions**, the clause begins with an **auxiliary** like *do*, *is*, or *have*.
 ▸ *Have* you heard about dinosaurs and how fast they used to run?
 ▸ *Did* Tyrannosaurus Rex run faster than today's footballers?

Or you can begin with a form of the **main verb** be (*is*, *are*, *was*, *were* etc).
 ▸ *Were* dinosaurs faster than scientists previously thought?

The second type of question is a request for **information** – you need more than a *yes* or a *no* in reply.

These are called **wh-questions**, because the clause begins with a **question word** like *who*, *which*, *what*, *whose*, *when*, *where*, *why* and *how*.
 ▸ *What* is the world's sleepiest mammal?
 ▸ *Which* snake can kill an elephant?
 ▸ *How* can you tell the age of a tree?
 ▸ *Why* doesn't an armadillo need poison?

 In text books and non-fiction, writers often use a question as a section **heading**, then they answer it underneath. This is quite a good way of organizing your writing.

Why is the Earth unique?
The Earth is the only one of the planets in the solar system that is able to sustain life ...

Clauses

❖ **Activity 11 Question words**
Match the two halves of these questions.

1	Who	**a** could a dinosaur run?
2	Which animals	**b** is a deciduous tree?
3	Where	**c** are some flowers red?
4	How	**d** use camouflage for protection?
5	How long ago	**e** invented the thermometer?
6	What	**f** was the wheel invented?
7	How fast	**g** did Roman merchants weigh things?
8	Why	**h** does gold come from?

Do you know the answers to any of the questions?

 You often ask questions when you don't expect an answer at all (though you may get one!). These are often called **rhetorical** questions.

> *Have you gone completely mad / nuts / barmy?*
> *Which bit of the word 'no' don't you understand?*
> *What did your last servant die of?*

People use this kind of question to make a joke or tease someone. Of course, there are more serious rhetorical questions.

> *I knew Jan would get all the headlines. What else did you think would happen?*
> *How do they expect us to sit down and talk to them when they behave like this?*

People often use this kind of question when they want to emphasize a point and get a supportive response of some kind from their listener.

Making a statement into a question: question tags

A **question tag** is a shortened clause that you add to the end of a statement to make it into a question.

You use question tags mostly in conversations, usually because you want your listener to agree with you or confirm your statement.

> He's a great player, *isn't he?*   Yes, he is.

You form a question tag by using an auxiliary, modal, or the main verbs *be* and *have*. You use a pronoun to refer back to the subject of the clause.

> *You are looking* for a job, **aren't you?**
> Oh well, *we can manage* somehow, **can't we?**

When the main clause is **positive**, you usually use a **negative tag**, and when the clause is negative, you usually use a positive tag.

> These trousers *are* a wee bit too tight, **aren't** they?
> You *haven't* met my father, **have** you?

If there is no auxiliary in the main clause, you add *do, does* or *didn't*, according to tense.

> The evidence never *lies*, **does** it?

❖ **Activity 12 Question tags**
Add suitable question tags to make these statements into questions, using the words below and a pronoun.

don't   won't   has   did   didn't

1 Dreams do come true, _____ ?

2 I mean, we never quarrelled or anything, _____ ?

3 'Someone will come to rescue us, _____ ?' she whispered.

4 'You believed me, _____ ?' she cried passionately.

5 He hasn't had any problem with his eyes, _____ ?

Standard and non-standard: Some people use *innit* as a general question tag, as in

✗ *'I followed you up there, innit?'*

You should avoid this in situations where it is important for you to speak standard English.

Imperatives

Imperatives are used to give commands and instructions. They are used on packaging, road signs and appliances, and in manuals, recipes, advertisements, promotions and exam papers.

- ▸ *Come* here!
- ▸ *Don't argue* with me.
- ▸ *Do not turn* upside down. (printed on bottom of dessert box!)
- ▸ *Do not iron* clothes on body. (on packaging for an iron)
- ▸ *Give way* to oncoming vehicles (road sign)
- ▸ *Pull* the plastic tab to activate the batteries. (manual)
- ▸ *Season* the cod and *place* in a shallow dish. (recipe)
- ▸ *Look* for the mark of quality.
- ▸ *Win* a gourmet weekend for two in Cornwall!
- ▸ *Explain* the processes by which water is made safe to drink.

Note that you don't always use the imperative for commands, instructions, etc. You can use a question to be more polite, or a statement to give instructions.

> **Could** you **explain** that again?
> You **should turn off** the power supply when the unit is not in use.

Types of clause: main and subordinate
There may be one, two, three or more clauses in a sentence. All clauses are either **main** or **subordinate**.

Main clauses
A main clause is a clause that can stand alone.

You can link two or more main clauses together and make a longer sentence using *and*, *but* or *or*. The clauses are equally important in the sentence.

    1 I tried to phone Andra, **2** but the line was busy.

Sentences like this are called **compound sentences**.

Subordinate clauses
A subordinate clause cannot stand alone.

    ? As I was going to St Ives
    ? When drops of hydrochloric acid were added

These don't make much sense, as you don't know what happened next. You need a **main clause** to give you that information.

    1 As I was going to St Ives, **2** I met a man with seven wives.
    1 When drops of hydrochloric acid were added, **2** the solution began to change colour.

You can link a main clause with a subordinate clause using subordinating conjunctions like *while* or *because*. The subordinate clause is less important than the main clause in the sentence.

1 Tamaki tried to write letters to him in English **2** because he didn't speak a word of Japanese.

Sentences like this are called **complex sentences**.

> **Did you know...?** You can use a subordinate clause on its own when you are answering a question.
>
> *Why was the archaeologist upset?*
> ✓ *Because his job was in ruins.*

❖ **Activity 13 Subordinate clauses**
Underline the subordinate clauses in these sentences.

1 Whenever there was an argument, Tom clammed up.

2 We went skateboarding if the weather was fine.

3 I worked hard on my fitness levels so that I'd be ready to play.

4 Though she was brought up in Singapore, she never learned Chinese.

Non-finite subordinate clauses

A subordinate clause is either **finite** or **non-finite**. A main clause is always finite. This means that the verb tells you **who** or **what** is doing something (the subject) and **when** they are doing it (past, present or future).

This is a **finite** main clause:
▸ Some flatfish can change the pattern and colour of their skin.

Some flatfish tells you what is doing the action, and *can change* tells you that this is true now, at present.

The next one is a **non-finite** subordinate clause:
▸ to suit the pattern and colour of the seabed

This does not make sense, as there is no subject. So you don't know who or what is the 'doer', and the verb doesn't tell you when this is happening. However, if you put the two clauses together, the sentence makes sense:

✓ **1** Flatfish can change the pattern and colour of their skin **2** to suit the pattern and colour of the seabed.

 Punctuation: When you begin a complex sentence with a non-finite subordinate clause, you put a comma between it and the main clause to make your meaning clearer.

✓ *Having lived abroad for so long, I'd forgotten how awful the TV ads are.*

❖ **Activity 14 Non-finite clauses**
Underline the non-finite clauses in these sentences.

1 When using brown or wholemeal flour, you often need a little more water to give you an elastic dough.

2 By 4000 BC, Sumerian merchants were travelling far and wide, trading food, cloth, pots and knives.

3 Invented during World War II, napalm became especially notorious in the Vietnam war.

Subordinate clauses 1: adverbial clauses

Three major types of subordinate clause are **adverbial clauses, relative clauses** and **report clauses**.

These are the main kinds of **adverbial clause**.

Time clauses

Time clauses answer the question 'when?'. They link events or situations into a sequence of some sort.

▸ Pine-cones grow hard and brown *after they are pollinated*.
▸ He dominated the race *until he blew his left rear tyre on the 51st lap*.

Clauses

▸ England face another match at Old Trafford **before heading for Germany**.

▸ **Having beaten the Olympic champion earlier in the year**, his hopes were high.

 Standard and non-standard: Can you tell what is wrong with this sentence?

> ✗ *Walking back home yesterday, a car mounted the pavement in front of me.*

This sounds as if it is the car that was walking home. You assume the subject of both clauses is the same, but here it isn't. It would be better to say:

> ✓ *While I was walking back home yesterday, a car...*
> ✓ *Walking back home yesterday, I saw a car...*

Place clauses

Place clauses answer the question 'where?'.

▸ **Where butterflies are disappearing**, nature in general is in trouble.

❖ **Activity 15 Time and place clauses**

Match the subordinate clauses 1–5 with main clauses a–e. The capital letters tell you which comes first.

1 Whene'er you meet a crocodile,   **a** they are bombarded with junk.

2 until the cows come home.   **b** he's ready for his dinner! (poem – anon)

3 As soon as he saw them   **c** We can argue about this

4 When the going gets tough,   **d** the tough go shopping.

5 Wherever children go,   **e** he yelled and waved wildly.

Conditional clauses

Conditional clauses tell you about possible actions or situations and the main clause tells you about their consequences.

- ▸ **If a tap is dripping**, it probably needs a new washer.
- ▸ The area could be under water by the end of the century **unless something is done**.
- ▸ **If we don't tackle global warming**, the planet will be in trouble.
- ▸ I would be very disappointed **if he was not included in the team**.
- ▸ I would be very surprised **if she moved over to Hollywood**.
- ▸ **If a person could die of embarrassment**, I'd be dead.
- ▸ She would have been blamed **if things had gone wrong**.
- ▸ Would you mind **if I tape our conversation?**

There are many very frequent *if* clauses.

If all goes well …	**If all else fails …**
If you can …	**If you're lucky …**
If it hadn't been for …	**If that's the case …**

 When you give someone advice, you often use *if I were you* or *if I was you*. *If I were you* is much more common, and some people think that *if I was you* is wrong.

*I wouldn't eat too many sweets **if I were you**, Melanie.*

❖ **Activity 16 Conditional clauses**

These are all proverbs or bits of poems. Match the subordinate clauses 1–4 with main clauses a–d.

1 If pigs could fly,

    a beggars would ride.

2 If wishes were horses,

    b I'd fly a pig, to foreign countries small and big.

3 If all the world was paper, and all the sea was ink, and all the trees were bread and cheese,

    c don't take a stick and poke him.

4 If you should meet a crocodile,

    d what would we have to drink?

Clauses

Reason clauses
Reason clauses answer the question 'why?'. They give you information about why something happens or should happen. The main clause tells you the result.

> **Because energy is so important**, it has to be a central part of government policy.

> You need a car to explore the area, **since public transport is not available**.

> I went indoors and shut the door, **realizing that I had to be alone**.

Purpose clauses
Purpose clauses answer the question 'what for?'. They give you information about what someone is or was aiming to do. The main clause tells you how they achieve that result.

> Maisie stood on a chair **so that she could climb into the attic**.

> The animals eat and eat and eat, **so that they'll be fat for winter**.

> She swallowed the cat **to catch the bird**...

> I had extra lessons from my dad **so as to catch up in maths**.

Result clauses
Result clauses tell you the result of an action or event. The main clause usually gives an explanation or reason. It must come after the main clause.

> We're in Tokyo at the moment **so we haven't heard the details from the UK**.

Contrast clauses
Contrast clauses explain how two situations or ideas are somehow in contrast to each other.

> **Whilst children know how to use the internet and mobile phones**, they know little about where their food comes from.

> I'll listen to what you have to say **even though I know I'll disagree**.

> They exclude the victims of bullying for 'health and safety' reasons, **while failing to tackle the initial problem**.

❖ Activity 17 Different adverbial clauses
Match the main clauses 1–8 with subordinate clauses a–h.

1 I repeated what I had said

a as long as the temperature remained below minus 20 degrees in the morning.

2 We left home early

b in case anyone had misunderstood.

3 Pedestrians are taking increasing risks

c whereas now we just flick on a switch and expect everything to work.

4 State schools in Moscow told students to stay at home

d so that the sunlight may not touch him.

5 The calculations took over an hour,

e because she was so bad at sums.

6 In days gone by we filled our coal scuttle or collected wood for the fire,

f even though she'd eaten breakfast only an hour ago.

7 She unpacked her banana sandwiches,

g in order to cross the road.

8 It is in one of these vaults that the Count sleeps during the day

h so as to beat the traffic.

Subordinate clauses 2: relative clauses
Another major type of subordinate clause is the **relative clause**. Relative clauses come after a noun or noun group and give you more information about it.

You usually begin a relative clause with a **relative pronoun**. You use *who* or *that* if the noun is a person, and *which* or *that* if it is a thing.

> Pegasus was the Greek hero *who beheaded the terrible she-monster Medusa*.

Clauses

> ‣ They were the same teenagers *that I had often seen there*.
> ‣ She peered into the ominous fog *that blanketed the frozen river*.
> ‣ Ridha looked at me with an expression *which could only be called stony*.

Whose must be followed by a noun.

> ‣ There was an old person of Dutton, *whose head was as small as a button*.

 When you write **definitions**, you often use a relative clause.

A paragraph is a group of sentences that are related to each other.

❖ **Activity 18 Definitions**
The sentences are all definitions. Make suggestions for completing the relative clauses, using your general knowledge.

1 A carnivore is an animal **that** _____.

2 A herbivore is an animal **that** _____.

3 Carbon dioxide is the gas **that** _____.

4 An astronomer is a person **who** _____.

5 Your heart is the organ **which** _____.

When a relative pronoun is the **object** of the relative clause, you can usually omit it.

> ‣ I remembered the little crooked bridge *(that) I had walked over in Shanghai*.

You can use *whom* only as the **object** of a relative clause, but its use is becoming rarer.

> ‣ My grandfather married a woman *whom he loved dearly*.

You can use a **preposition** before the relative pronouns *whom* and *which*.

> ‣ The Take That star was reunited with the band *with which he made his name in the early 90s*.
> ‣ She's the girl *with whom I share my lunch*.

But using a preposition before a relative pronoun sounds quite formal. Usually you can just put the preposition at the end and use *who* or *that* instead.

> ▸ She's the girl ***who I share my lunch with***.
> ▸ I have some jobs around the house ***that I have to attend to***.
> ⁇ I have some jobs around the house to which I have to attend.

> **Standard and non-standard:** Teachers used to say that you shouldn't put a preposition at the end of a sentence. You can safely ignore this advice!

There are two main types of relative clause, **defining** and **non-defining**.

Defining relative clauses

Defining relative clauses give you essential information about a person or thing. They tell you the particular thing that the main clause refers to, so they cannot usually be omitted.

❖ **Activity 19 Defining relative clauses (1)**

Fill in the gaps using **who**, **whom**, **that**, **which**, or **whose**. If the clause doesn't need a relative pronoun, put '0' in the gap. There may be more than one possibility.

1 Termites build homes _____ **are as elaborate as a modern tower block**.

2 You're just the person _____ **I wanted to talk to**.

3 The ancient Egyptians used paper _____ **was made from papyrus reed**.

4 He had a daughter _____ **hobby was collecting ancient coins**.

5 She drew a picture of the creature _____ **she had seen**.

Clauses

❖ **Activity 20 Defining relative clauses (2)**
In the sentences below, find the beginning of the relative clause and insert the missing relative pronoun, using λ.

1 People thought the footprints were those of a big cat had escaped from the zoo.

2 There were things going on for I could find no logical explanation.

3 Mrs Twit had a glass eye was always looking the other way.

4 Two of Mum's close relations died recently, including the cousin to she'd been very close.

5 Anand had no words could adequately express his rage.

Non-defining relative clauses

Non-defining relative clauses give you extra information. They could be omitted, and you would still know which particular thing the main clause refers to.

▸ He has a large cheetah and a baboon, *which wander freely over his grounds*.

▸ There was an old man of the Cape,
   Who possessed a large Barbary Ape
   (Edward Lear; completed below)

Some non-defining relative clauses refer to an entire situation or event rather than a person or thing.

▸ But the Ape one dark night set the house all alight,
   Which burned that old man of the Cape.

 Punctuation: You usually have to put a comma before a non-defining relative clause.

   ✗ *She lit two slender perfumed candles which she put on the window-sill.*

✓ *She lit two slender perfumed candles,* **which she put on the window-sill**.

Standard and non-standard: You can't use *that* in non-defining relative clauses.

✓ *Debbie opened her eyes,* **which flashed as she stared straight at Ramesh**.

✗ *Debbie opened her eyes, that flashed as she stared straight at Ramesh.*

❖ **Activity 21 Non-defining relative clauses**
Fill in the gaps using **who**, **whom**, **which**, or **whose**. There may be more than one possibility.

1 A third man, _____ **address was not given**, also appeared before the court.

2 Most ancient civilizations were polytheistic, _____ **means that they worshipped more than one god**.

3 She never forgot about her father, **to** _____ **she wrote a letter every month**.

4 Early sea voyages were plagued by scurvy, _____ **was known as the seaman's curse**.

5 She introduced me to Shirin, _____ **she described as 'a very warm-hearted person'**.

Subordinate clauses 3: report clauses

A third type of subordinate clause is the **report clause.** You use a report clause when you are telling someone what you yourself or another person said or thought. This is often called **indirect speech.**

You begin a report clause with the linking word *that*. The most common verb in report clauses is *say*.

▸ He said ***that he was getting tired***.

▸ I promised ***that all my profits would go to charity***.

▸ She claimed ***that her classmates were bullying her***.

With common verbs like *say,* you can omit the word *that* from the report clause:

▸ I said ***I would clean up***, and I will.

Common verbs used in report clauses are:

say	*explain*	*mention*	*argue*	*admit*	*suggest*
claim	*insist*	*announce*	*state*	*deny*	*promise*

Some verbs have an **object** before the report clause:

▸ He ***told*** *his father* that he was going to his friend Vikram's house.

▸ She ***reminded*** *me* that I'd been late almost every day.

Sometimes you quote someone's exact words, using quote marks. This is often called **direct speech.**

▸ 'We***'re building*** a new climbing frame for the kids', she explained.

When you change this into a report clause (indirect speech), you often need to change the **tense** of the original statement, for example from present to past.

▸ She explained ***that they were building*** a new climbing frame for the kids.

 Standard and non-standard: There are some new ways of reporting speech that are becoming more and more common.

✗ *She asks if I use soap , and I'm like 'Come on, Mum, you know how it is with me and soap!'*

✗ *He looks at me and he goes 'I'm not afraid of anything'.*

You should not use these when you are writing or speaking standard English.

❖ **Activity 22 Report clauses**
Fill in the gaps using the verbs below.

informed   replied   denied   warn   promised   complains

1 He often _____ that he doesn't get the respect he deserves.

2 The council _____ that the repairs to the bridge would be completed by November.

3 Then she _____ me that her daughter was getting married.

4 His family and friends _____ that he had anything to do with terrorism.

5 The big tobacco companies failed to _____ consumers that smoking is harmful and addictive.

6 I asked her how she had got into the house and she _____ that Jemima had given her the keys.

Part 5

Sentences and sentence linking

Types of sentence

There are three major types of sentence: **simple**, **compound** and **complex**.

Simple sentences
Simple sentences consist of a single clause.
- I put on my coat.
- Did you have a good time yesterday?
- Try rebooting your machine.

> **Did you know…?** Newspaper headlines are often simple sentences, but with some words left out. Here are some famous ones, which all have two meanings as a result.
>
> *STUDY OF OBESITY LOOKS FOR LARGER TEST GROUP*
>
> *ENRAGED COW INJURES FARMER WITH AXE*
>
> *DRUNK DRIVERS PAID $1,000 IN 1984*

Compound sentences
Compound sentences contain two or more main clauses that are linked by the **co-ordinating conjunctions** *and*, *but*, or *or*. The sentence could be separated into simple sentences, because each clause could stand alone.

1 I put on my coat **2** and I walked in the rain over the hills.
- ✓ I put on my coat.
- ✓ I walked in the rain over the hills.

❖ **Activity 1 Compound sentences**
Match the clauses 1–6 with the clauses a–f to make compound sentences, and insert **and** or **but** between the two main clauses.

Types of sentence

↘

1 Mrs Twit may have been ugly and she may have been beastly,

a go back to the African jungle where they came from.

2 Mr Twit caught the birds

b Tamaki found quite a few things she could try on.

3 The kitchen window opened easily,

c she was not stupid.

4 Muggle-Wump and his family longed to escape from the cage in Mr Twit's garden

d Mrs Twit cooked them.

5 Her bare feet ached from running on concrete,

e she ignored the pain.

6 The shop wasn't large,

f climbing in turned out to be tricky.

Omitting words

When you link clauses together in a compound sentence, you can often omit some of the words that you have said before (**ellipsis**). The clauses in the next example 'share' the same subject *He* and the auxiliary *had*:

1 He <u>had</u> stopped **2** and towed her back to the garage.

You don't need to say *He had stopped and he had towed her back to the garage.*

When you use *or* as a co-ordinating conjunction, you very often use ellipsis of some kind.

1 Downstairs my parents were talking **2** or playing cards.

You can link quite a lot of clauses together, putting the co-ordinating conjunction before the last clause.

1 Marwan coughed, **2** seemed about to say something, **3** but remained silent.

1 Nessie, the oldest girl, **2** could sew, **3** mend, **4** cook, **5** clean, **6** and look after the little ones.

1 He wasn't smiling, **2** chuckling **3** or joking any longer.

When you use ellipsis you must make sure the meaning is right. This is a headline that went wrong (from The Independent).

> *AT LEAST 3 BRITONS INJURED AND 88 CONFIRMED DEAD IN PLANE CRASH*

Although the headline might suggest it, 88 British people did not die in the crash. Could you rephrase the headline to give the correct meaning?

Politicians and other people who speak in public often choose not to use ellipsis. Instead they repeat the whole of each clause, because it makes them sound very emphatic.

> ▸ We shall go on to the end, we shall fight in France, we shall fight on the seas and oceans, we shall fight with growing confidence and growing strength in the air, we shall defend our Island, whatever the cost may be, we shall fight on the beaches, we shall fight on the landing grounds, we shall fight in the fields and in the streets, we shall fight in the hills; we shall never surrender ...
> (Winston Churchill, in a World War II broadcast)

 There are eleven clauses in the extract above, but it is not the whole sentence. There are four more long clauses, and the whole sentence contains 141 words! That is how the speech is written, but of course it was originally spoken, and there were lots of pauses.

You should avoid very long sentences in your writing. You will probably come across them in your literature classes, however, especially if you read 19th-century writers like Charles Dickens.

Did you know...? In literature and especially poetry, writers often put *and* between words. It gives rhythm to a sentence.

> *She swallowed the bird to catch the spider*
> *That wiggled **and** jiggled **and** tickled inside her.*

Do you know how this children's rhyme begins?

Writers also repeat the conjunction to give emphasis and have a stronger effect on the reader.

> *The cavalry were climbing **or** swimming **or** running **or** riding away from the battlefield.*

Types of sentence

❖ **Activity 2 Linking in compound sentences**
Put these words into the most natural order to make compound sentences. The first word is in the right place. Add commas where necessary.

Example:

The families / move / locally / from the area / and not / jobs / want to find / away

The families want to find jobs locally and not move away from the area.

1 He / her / steal / lie / not to / or / or / to other people / taught / be spiteful

2 People / cheering / singing / in / were / dancing / and / the streets

3 Gibb's staff / his family's / cater for / clean / and / cook / every need

4 The women / transport / on their heads / chop wood / and / must cook / heavy loads / clean

Complex sentences

Complex sentences also contain two or more clauses. However, they are linked in a different way. They may be linked by a **subordinating conjunction**. These are words like *because*, *when* and *whereas*.

In complex sentences, at least one clause is a main clause, with one or more subordinate clauses. These subordinate clauses would not be able to stand alone as simple sentences if you separate the longer sentence out.

In a complex sentence, a subordinate clause does not have to come after the main clause. It can come before it.

▸ A dog may start pawing the air *when it wants to play*.
▸ *When it wants to play*, it may start pawing the air.

▸ *Whilst living in France* she kept in close touch with her family.
▸ She kept in close touch with her family *whilst living in France*.

❖ **Activity 3 Complex sentences**
Put these words into the right order to make well-known proverbs, adding capital letters. They are all complex sentences.

1 angels / rush in / to tread / fools / fear / where

2 Rome / the Romans / do / do / when / as / in

3 a way / where / there's / there's / a will

4 chickens / your / count / until / hatched / don't / they're

5 away / play / when / the mice / the / will / cat's

6 until / to them / you / cross / bridges / your / don't / come

Do you know what these proverbs mean?

A sentence may be both compound and complex. This one has two clauses linked by *and*, then a subordinate clause beginning with *when*:

1 One morning she took out her glass eye **2 *and*** dropped it into Mr Twit's mug of beer **3 *when*** he wasn't looking.

❖ **Activity 4 Different types of sentence**
Say whether the sentences are simple, compound, or complex, or a mixture.

(1) .... Things cling to hairs, especially food. **(2)** Things like gravy go right in among the hairs and stay there. **(3)** You and I can wipe our smooth faces with a flannel and we quickly look more or less all right again, but the hairy man cannot do that. **(4)** We can also, if we are careful, eat our meals without spreading food all over our faces. **(5)** But not so the hairy man. **(6)** Watch carefully next time you see a hairy man eating his lunch and you will notice that even if he opens his mouth very wide, it is impossible for him to get a spoonful of beef-stew or ice-cream and chocolate sauce into it without leaving some of it on the hairs. **(7)** Mr Twit didn't even bother to open his mouth wide when he ate. **(8)** As a result (and because he never washed) there were always hundreds of bits of old breakfasts and lunches and suppers sticking to the hairs around his face.
(*The Twits*, by Roald Dahl)

Punctuation: When you link a lot of clauses together to make compound or complex sentences, you do not need a conjunction between every clause if the **subject** and **tense** are the same.

Josie shook her head, sighed loudly, and left the room.

But when these are different, or the idea you're expressing is different, you usually have to use a conjunction or a semicolon. Or you may put a full stop and start a new sentence.

This is wrong:

X *He didn't bother to keep his voice down, he thought Jaz didn't understand Bengali, she understood it perfectly, her family sometimes spoke it at home.*

This makes the meaning much clearer:

*He didn't bother to keep his voice down **because** he thought Jaz didn't understand Bengali. **But** she understood it perfectly; her family sometimes spoke it at home.*

The semicolon keeps the close connection between the last two clauses, but it means you don't need a conjunction.

Irregular sentences

There is another type of sentence. An irregular sentence is a sentence that is abnormal in some way. It may be a subordinate clause standing alone, or it may have no verb at all.

When you answer a question, you often use a subordinate clause on its own, because you are 'sharing' the making of a sentence with someone else.

▸ Why did she give her son so much junk food?
✓ To reward him for doing his homework.

You also see or hear a lot of irregular sentences in:

- adverts
- slogans
- headlines in newspapers, magazines, etc.
- catalogues
- instructions
- road signs

Irregular sentence – subordinate clause only
- Hand baked in Italy (advert)
- Because you're worth it (slogan)
- Flying in the face of well-known facts ('opinion' column)
- While stocks last (notice next to a 'special offer')

Irregular sentence – no verbs
- Cyprus. The year-round island. A welcoming destination (advert)
- Invasion of the human snails (magazine article about caravans)
- Cotton pintuck shirt. Semi-fitted shape. Full-length sleeves. Delicate pintuck detail on front. Mother-of-pearl buttons. (clothes catalogue)
- For indoor or outdoor use only (instruction on box of Christmas lights!)
- No hard shoulder for 500 yards (motorway sign)

❖ **Activity 5 Irregular sentences**
What do you think these 'irregular sentences' are and where might they be found?

1 Very soft zipped polo shirt with peachskin touch. Woven striped design

2 Melting ice cap triggering earthquakes

3 Tunisia, where ancient Carthage watches over the Mediterranean

4 The most important protest of our time

5 Accurate to the second! State-of-the-art analogue day date watch

6 Beer and cheer for the three lions of England

Linking sentences to make texts

You don't often use one sentence on its own. Usually you have to link sentences together to form paragraphs and connected texts. You use a wide range of words and phrases, called **sentence linkers**, to do this. Different ways of linking sentences are described below.

Connectives

You can use some adverbs and prepositional phrases, called **connectives**, to link sentences together and show the relationship between them.

Some connectives make a **contrast** between two sentences. The most useful are *however, but, nevertheless, instead* and *on the other hand*.

> A golfer saw 'a big cat, a big black panther' close to a rubbish bin, but was too shy to say anything. **However**, after a sleepless night he reported the sighting to a park supervisor.

There is a contrast here between the golfer being 'too shy to say anything' and his eventual report of seeing the 'big cat'.

Some connectives tell you that the second sentence gives **extra** information. The most useful are *moreover, besides, in addition, even so* and *also*.

> This upbeat story is perfect for reading aloud. **Besides**, kids can learn a lot from it.

The second sentence gives extra information about the 'story'.

Note that you could just connect these ideas in one sentence, using *and*:

> *This upbeat story is perfect for reading aloud, and kids can learn a lot from it.*

However, this doesn't work well as the two ideas are too different to be linked by *and*. The writer wanted to emphasize this, so he or she used a connective.

The connectives *for example* and *for instance* are very important, because you have to give examples a lot in your writing. These connectives signal that you are about to do so.

> ▸ Nowadays there are fewer opportunities for kids to burn off those calories. **For example**, in this area only a third of all children walk to school.

Some connectives signal that the second sentence is a **result** of an idea you expressed earlier. The most useful are *therefore*, *so*, *consequently* and *as a result*.

> ▸ The storm has left many without power and phone lines. **As a result**, reliable information is scarce.

Some connectives signal how the sentences are connected in time. For example, they tell you whether things happened before or after each other, or at the same time. The most useful are *then*, *afterwards*, *later*, *previously*, *meanwhile*, *now* and *immediately*.

> ▸ In August, Mario changed his will. **Previously**, he had left his estate to his sister and his two nephews; **now**, he left everything to Maria.

 Punctuation: You often put all these connectives at the beginning of the sentence, followed by a **comma**.

> *He arranged all his underwear and shirts perfectly by colour and size.* **Moreover,** *he imposed this system on his wife and children.*

When you use these connectives in the middle of a sentence, you should put commas before and after them.

> *The noise was very puzzling. It soon stopped,* **however,** *and the children could relax again.*

An exception is *also*, which is often used without a comma.

> *The girls set the table and washed up the dishes. We were* **also** *responsible for tidying our rooms.*

Linking sentences to make texts

 Punctuation: You can also use all these connectives after a **semicolon**. The bits before and after a semicolon are just like sentences (as you can see if you replace the connective with a full stop), but they are more closely linked.

> *This is a step in the right direction; **however**, in many ways it still doesn't go far enough.*

 Note that you should not add connectives if you do not need them. If the relationship between the sentences is quite clear, you don't need a connective.

> *Of course Justine would be there, helping out. I wondered why Daddy didn't do it, to free Justine.*

You could use *however* in the second sentence, but there is no need.

❖ Activity 6 Connectives

Fill in the gaps using the words below. Insert capital letters where necessary.

> **on the other hand   therefore   nevertheless   also**
> **for example   in addition**

1 She wasn't travelling with anybody, _____ nobody reported her missing during the cruise.

2 Often he'd go for hours without speaking at all. Maya, _____ , could not be silent.

3 Isabelle was rather enjoying her new fame, after so many years. _____ , she did not allow it to turn her head.

4 The pillows had been ripped apart, and feathers covered my bed, the floor, the table. The sheets were _____ ripped.

5 Many parents have to go to work, which limits the time they can spend with their children. _____ , children are involved in school and other activities.

6 Some countries have more efficient medical services than others. _____ , let's take a look at Cuba.

Showing a sequence

Other **sentence linkers** can be used in different ways. For example, you can use adverbs like *first* (or *firstly*), *secondly*, *thirdly*, *finally*, *next* and *then* to put your points in order. You often say right at the beginning how many points you are going to make.

> It was an outstanding game. ***Three main factors*** contributed to this. ***Firstly***, we had two teams in great form. ***Secondly***, all 34 players supported the abilities of their team-mates. ***Thirdly***, referee Steve Clark awarded just three penalties in the whole game.

In your writing, try to experiment with the more unfamiliar connectives and sequencing words. It will make your writing more expressive and interesting if you don't just use *and*, *then* and *because*.

> ✗ *It was an outstanding game because we had two teams in great form and all 35 players supported the abilities of their team-mates and Steve Clarke awarded only three penalties.*

Remember that if you say you are going to make three points or express three ideas, you must give exactly **three**, not four or two!

Showing your opinion or attitude

Sometimes you want to show your opinion of something or your attitude towards what you are saying.

You can give your **opinion** of what you are saying by using an adverb. Here are some useful ones.

fortunately	*luckily*	*unfortunately*	*sadly*
strangely enough	*oddly enough*		

These adverbs also help to link sentences together as you relate fact and opinion.

> I was always quite shy. ***Strangely enough***, not all actors are loudmouth show-offs who love charades.

> We ended up getting a lift home from a Japanese man from Dragon Gate who had never been to Detroit before. ***Fortunately***, his hobby was cartography, the study of maps.

Linking sentences to make texts

You can indicate your **attitude** to what you are saying or how strongly you believe it. Here are some useful adverbs and phrases for showing this.

obviously	*typically*	*apparently*	*of course*
actually	*in fact*	*probably*	*perhaps*
honestly	*naturally*	*personally*	*in my opinion*

Again, these adverbs can be used to organize your writing as you move between making statements and commenting or adding ideas.

> He looks as if he's wondering what's for dinner. ***Apparently***, he's not satisfied that he's just cleaned out our fridge.

> The boy was only an amateur, but he wasn't bad. ***In fact***, he hardly missed a thing.

> Most people think of sheds as damp dumping grounds full of spiders and old toys. ***Personally***, I am a huge fan of sheds – my first office was one.

❖ **Activity 7 Showing your opinion or attitude**
These sentences are all linked to previous ideas. Begin the sentences using the adverbs below. Choose the one that fits best.

**Unfortunately   Naturally   Fortunately
Actually   Sadly   Typically**

1 _____ , now I come to think of it, I did notice this morning that my trousers weren't quite so tight.

2 _____ , global warming is melting the polar bear's world and along with it his chance to feed, reproduce and ultimately survive.

3 _____ , I understand and sympathize. I've been there myself.

4 _____ , January and February are the worst months for flooding.

5 _____ , there is now a vaccine that will prevent girls from getting cervical cancer.

6 _____ , Hollywood still glamorizes smoking.

Linking sentences to make texts

❖ **Activity 8 Different sentence linkers**
Fill in the gaps using the words and phrases below. Insert capital
letters where necessary.

> **naturally   instead   then   next   moreover
> oddly enough   probably   for example**

1 To insert an arrow into your text, go to the toolbar and select
Insert, Symbol. _____ , scroll down until you find the
arrow you want. Press Insert, and _____ close the box.

2 The men sit around the fire and tell hunting stories.
_____ , one tells how he killed a crocodile that was as
long as the river is wide. _____ , everyone knows that the
stories are greatly exaggerated , but it is entertaining.

3 Selina knew she should have been editing a glossy fashion
magazine in Manhattan. _____ , she was sitting in a poky
little office next to Sammy's barber shop.

4 Ever since then, he had made one mistake after another.
_____ he had just made another one by missing this
golden opportunity.

5 _____ , 72 percent of the American public does not
know that plastic is made from petroleum products, primarily
oil. _____ , 40 per cent of the respondents believe that
plastic will biodegrade at some point.

Referring back

Another way of linking sentences together is to refer back to an idea you
have already expressed, so as to organize your writing stage by stage. This
way you make your writing more **cohesive** (which just means that it hangs
together well).

Using personal pronouns

You can use personal pronouns to create a cohesive text. You use a pronoun to refer back to a person or idea you mentioned before. In this way you save space and avoid repetition as well.

The use of pronouns creates **reference chains** in a text. There may be two or three of these in the same text.

> The brown hen had been listening to this conversation and chuckling to **herself**. 'There are a lot of things Porky doesn't know about life,' **she** thought. '**He**'s really a very innocent little pig. **He** trusts the farmer and his wife. But **they** are planning to eat **him** for Christmas, and **he** doesn't have the slightest suspicion!'

There are three chains here:
> the brown hen → **herself** → **she**
> Porky → **He** → **He** → **him** → **he**
> the farmer and his wife → **they**

You must be very careful to make your pronoun reference chains quite clear. When there is more than one person of the same sex involved, they can get muddled, and you lose track of who is who.

*Mrs Slaski loved her daughter. **She** could not understand why **she** did not want to see her, although **she** wanted to stand by **her** during **her** recovery.*

It is not quite clear whether the second *she* and the first *her* refer to *Mrs Slaski* or *her daughter*. If your reference chain gets muddled, repeat a noun, or better, use a different noun.

*… **She** could not understand why **the child** did not want to see **her** …*

Using 'this' and 'that'

You can also refer back to previous sentences using the demonstrative pronouns *this* and *that*.

These often refer back to a whole statement or situation, which may be one sentence or more. So they are very useful in organizing a paragraph or text.

> It made them giddy standing on their heads for hours on end. But Mr Twit didn't care about **that**.

▷ 'I'll go back to my room in a little while,' said Janny. Neither of us could think of any reply to **this**.

Using 'so' and 'not'

You can use *so* or *not* to refer back to the action, statement or idea expressed in the previous sentence, often with the verb *do* + *so* or *not*.

▷ She climbed the steps carefully and finally reached the top. As she **did so**, she heard the piercing cry of a child.

▷ Motorists have to treat other drivers with courtesy. If they **do not**, people get angry and accidents happen.

You often use *so* and *not* to connect parts of a conversation, especially with the verbs *think* and *believe*.

▷ 'You'll regret this,' Liz said defiantly. 'I **don't think so**,' he replied, a sneer on his face.

▷ 'I wonder if I've been of any use?' thought Hasan. 'I'd really like to **think so**.'

If so and *if not* are also often used to refer back.

▷ She is probably a good person at heart. **If not**, she's at least struggling to be good.

❖ **Activity 9 Referring back**
Fill in the gaps using the words below.

this   it   we   do   so   she   that   he   her

1 In the past Terry and I had always worked through our problems. This time _____ would just have to _____ again.

2 'I may seem to be sentimental, Jessie, but basically I'm a practical man. You do understand _____ don't you?' 'Why, of course!' _____ replied, looking surprised.

3 'I think they'll come down through the mountains and attack us.' Masha's voice sounded shaky as she said _____ .

4 'Jetta! Jetta!' called Ginny. The tabby tomcat saw her and ran to
_____ . _____ dropped a dead mouse at her feet . All his life
Jetta had been bringing his human friends such gifts. But did they
appreciate _____ ? Never.

Punctuation: Look at the punctuation of the **speech** in Activity
9. Generally, when you report what someone says, the closing
speech marks ('**...**' or " **...**") go **outside** the other punctuation.

"You understand what I mean, don't you?" Jem asked.

*"Oh, I couldn't take any money," he said. "You're in the country
now; folks help each other out."*

The exception is when only part of a clause is a report of what
someone said. Then the speech marks come first.

*At around 12.30 he said he was "popping out for a bite of lunch",
and no-one has seen him since!*

Closing speech
marks usually go
outside other
punctuation

Linking sentences logically

The important thing to remember in your writing is that when you connect sentences, each must follow **logically** from the last.

If you don't use any linker, the link must be clear without one.

 If you do use a linker, it must be the right one. There is a difference in meaning between *instead* and *on the other hand*, for example:

> ? *They drew lots and it fell to Abu Yusef to shoot first. He let fly an arrow with impressive force. He didn't hit the bird. On the other hand, his arrow struck the thin cord that tethered the bird, severing it. The pigeon flew free.*

> ✓ *They drew lots and it fell to Abu Yusef to shoot first. He let fly an arrow with impressive force **but** didn't hit the bird. **Instead**, his arrow struck the thin cord that tethered the bird, severing it, **so that** the pigeon flew free.*

The **tenses** should be logically related too – make sure that you have a good reason for switching from one tense to another. The reader should find it easy to know whether you are talking about the past or the present or the future.

 Here the tense changes are not logical:

> ✗ *Finally Rusti was forced to admit they have missed their turning. The others insist that they go back and he agrees. So they turned and begin to retrace their steps.*

This is better:

> ✓ *Finally Rusti was forced to admit they had missed their turning. The others insisted that they go back and he agreed. So they turned and began to retrace their steps.*

See also Part 1, page 23.

Linking sentences to make texts

❖ **Activity 10 Linking sentences logically**
What is wrong with the following paragraph? Rewrite a better version on a piece of paper. You will need to do these things:

1 Change **two** wrongly used linkers.

2 Remove **one** unnecessary linker.

3 Change **five** verb tenses.

They were now staring at a sagging greenhouse and an old cucumber frame. Every pane of glass of both is broken. Moreover, there was a gorgeous fresh tangy smell in the air. At first Paula can't work out where it was coming from. She sniffed a couple of times, wondering. Afterwards she's laughing and looked down at their feet. In fact they are standing on an overgrown carpet of mint, the scent of which rose to their nostrils in the cold morning mist. Paula thinks it was sad to see so much neglect.

Varying clause and sentence types

Good writers vary the clause and sentence types they use. A good text contains different sentence types, for example:

- short simple sentences
- compound sentences
- complex sentences
- active sentences
- passive sentences

 When you use two or three different types of clause and sentence in a piece of writing, it flows more freely and is more interesting for your reader.

This bit of text (not a complete paragraph) is quite varied:

1 After tea they went walking in the grounds, which were looking charming. **2** Bonelli had a passion for trees and let them spread wherever they liked. **3** Wild strawberries poked up through the grass. **4** Charlotte went to find her sister, along the river and through a tangle of blackberry bushes. **5** She heard steps behind her and the elder girl caught her up.

1 is a complex sentence (*which* begins a subordinate clause).
2 is both compound and complex (*...and ... wherever ...*).
3 is a simple sentence with an adverbial (*through the* grass).
4 is a simple sentence with two adverbials (*along the river* and *through a tangle of blackberry bushes*).
5 is a compound sentence (*... and ...*).

❖ **Activity 11 Varying clause and sentence types**
This bit of text is dull and stilted because it consists of short simple sentences. First read the passage.

1 School started again in September. **2** My brother and I took a different route to school on our bicycles. **3** The reason was simple greed. **4** In the woods there were lots of blackberries. **5** We ate as many as we could. **6** We forgot about the time. **7** We'd often arrive late at school. **8** We had to run into the classroom with blackberry stains. **9** We didn't get into trouble. **10** Everyone in the class had been doing the same thing.

Now do the following to improve the passage:

a Link the sentences to form compound and complex sentences, using connectives and other linkers. Try to end up with a maximum of seven sentences instead of ten.

b In **4**, expand the noun group 'the woods' to tell your reader where the woods are, and expand 'lots of blackberries' to say what the blackberries were like.

c In **8**, expand the noun group 'blackberry stains' to tell your reader more about them.

Language glossary

abstract noun

An abstract noun is a noun that refers to ideas, qualities, situations and experiences, such as *theory*, *strength*, *hope*, *life*, *problem* and *success*.

▶ See also concrete noun, proper noun.

active verb chain

An active verb chain occurs in a clause whose subject is the person or thing doing the action or responsible for a situation. *He left the house. She has decided. The ice is melting.*

▶ See also passive verb chain.

adjective

An adjective is a word that tells you more about a noun. There are two main types: 1) adjectives that tell you about the <u>qualities</u> of a person or thing, such as *fantastic*, *tiny*, *clean* and *tasty* and 2) adjectives that refer to a <u>kind</u> of person or thing (often called **classifying** adjectives) such as *female*, *personal*, *global* and *electronic*.

adjective group

An adjective group is an adjective combined with other words such as adverbs or prepositional phrases, such as *perfectly capable*, *fairly cheap*, and *allergic to peanuts*. The adjective is the **head** of the adjective group.

adverb

An adverb is a word that gives more information about when, where, why or in what circumstances something happens or is done, such as *dangerously*, *suddenly*, *occasionally* and *completely*. Some adverbs tell you more about an adjective, such as *utterly useless*.

Language glossary

The main kinds of adverb are **manner adverbs**, like *beautifully*; **time adverbs**, like *immediately*; **place adverbs**, like *indoors*; **aspect adverbs**, like *psychologically*; **sentence adverbs**, like *however*; and **degree adverbs**, like *very*.

adverbial

An adverbial is the part of the clause that gives you information about time, place, manner, and any other circumstances. Adverbials are usually adverbs or prepositional phrases, such as *very well* and *on Sundays*. (The term **adjunct** is often used instead.)

▶ See also subject, verb, object, complement.

adverbial clause

An adverbial clause is a subordinate clause containing a verb. The clause gives you more information about the event in the main clause. Different types of adverbial clause are

- **time clauses** like *when I was young*
- **place clauses** like *wherever you like*
- **conditional clauses** like *if you're lucky*
- **reason clauses** like *because it was snowing*
- **purpose clauses** like *so as to pass the test*
- **result clauses** like *so it all ended in disaster*
- **contrast clauses** like *even though I disagree*

apostrophe

An apostrophe is the punctuation mark '. You use it to indicate possession or relation, as in *Ali's* book, *life's* problems, or to indicate missing letters in contractions such as *I'm*, *it's*, *hasn't* and *wouldn't*.

article

Articles are a kind of determiner. The **definite article** is *the*, and the **indefinite article** is *a* (or *an* before a vowel).

auxiliary verb

There are three auxiliary verbs, *do* (*does*, *did*), *be* (*is*, *are*, *was*, *were*, *being*, *been*), and *have* (*has*, *having*, *had*). You use them with different main verbs to form verb chains such as *didn't go*, *was thinking* and *have* finished. (The term **helping verb** is sometimes used instead.)

clause

A clause is a group of words that expresses an event or a situation. It usually contains a subject and a verb. There are two principal types: 1) **main clauses**, which can stand alone, such as *I phoned Andra*, and 2) **subordinate clauses**, which are linked to a main clause, such as *because it was her birthday*.

closed class

The closed classes are **pronouns** like *I* and *me*, **determiners** like *the* and *this*, **prepositions** like *to* and *from* and **conjunctions** like *and* and *because*. There is a fixed number of words in each of these classes, and new ones very rarely come into the language.

▶ See also **open class**.

collective noun

A collective noun is a noun that refers to a group of people or things, for example, *team*, *staff*. It can be followed by a singular or a plural verb. *The team **is** ready. The team **are** ready.*

collocation; collocate

Collocation is often defined as 'the company words keep'. This means that words do not combine together randomly, but are usually found with other particular words. For example, you **make** *a* **choice** or **set** an **example**. You **keep a low profile** rather than a *small profile*; you talk about a **can** of **worms** not a *tin*; you say that something is **a grey area** rather than *a grey region*. The verb is **collocate**; for example **hand** collocates with **lend** in the phrase **lend a hand**, but not with *borrow*, as you do not *borrow a hand*.

comparative adjective/adverb

The comparative form of an adjective or adverb is the form you use to compare two things, people, situations, or changes over time, as in *a **cheaper** solution, a **more popular** leader, **better** than before, **more quickly***.

▶ See also **superlative adjective/adverb**.

Language glossary

complement

The complement is the part of the clause that identifies the subject or tells you more about the subject. It comes after a link verb like *be*, *seem*, and *appear*. Complements are noun groups or adjective groups. *She's **a sensible person**. She seems **very confident**.*

▶ See also subject, verb, object, adverbial.

complex sentence

A complex sentence consists of a main clause and one or more subordinate clauses, as in ***I phoned Andra because it was her birthday***. The clauses are often linked by subordinating conjunctions like *because*, *when*, *whereas* and *if*.

▶ See also compound sentence, simple sentence.

compound sentence

A compound sentence consists of two or more main clauses linked by the co-ordinating conjunctions *and*, *but* and *or*.

▶ See also complex sentence, simple sentence.

compound word

A compound word is a 'multi-word' that consists of two or more words used together and considered as a unit. They include nouns like ***flowchart***, ***makeup***, ***light year***, ***horse-riding*** and ***public transport***, as well as adjectives like ***mass-produced***, ***computer-literate*** and ***accident-prone***.

concrete noun

A concrete noun is a noun that refers to a person or thing that you can see, hear or touch, like ***boat***, ***garden***, ***computer*** and ***shoe***.

▶ See also abstract noun, proper noun.

conjunction

▶ See co-ordinating conjunction, subordinating conjunction.

connective

A connective is a word or phrase that you can use to link sentences together and show the relationship between them. Connectives are usually **adverbs** like **_however_** and **_moreover_**, or **prepositional phrases** like **_on the other hand_**.

▸ See also **sentence linker**.

consonant

The consonants are the letters **_b_**, **_c_**, **_d_**, **_f_**, **_g_**, **_h_**, **_j_**, **_k_**, **_l_**, **_m_**, **_n_**, **_p_**, **_q_**, **_r_**, **_s_**, **_t_**, **_v_**, **_w_**, **_x_**, **_y_**, and **_z_**. The letter h often sounds like a **vowel**, as in _honest_. So does the letter y, as in _happy_.

▸ See also **vowel**.

contraction

A contraction is a reduced form of a subject plus the verbs _be_ or _have_, as in **_she's_** _singing_ or **_I've_** _finished_. The full forms are _she is_ and _I have_. A contraction is also a reduced form of a verb plus _not_, as in _you_ **_didn't_** _listen_.

co-ordinating conjunction

The co-ordinating conjunctions **_and_**, **_but_** and **_or_** link words, groups, chains and **main clauses**.

▸ See also **subordinating conjunction**.

count noun

A count noun is a noun that has both singular and plural forms, for example **_boy/boys_**, **_fox/foxes_**, and **_country/countries_**. (The term **countable noun** is often used instead.)

▸ See also **uncount noun**.

defining relative clause

A defining relative clause gives you essential information about a person or thing, and cannot usually be omitted. It usually begins with a **relative pronoun**, with no comma before it. _She's the girl_ **_who lives across the park_**.

▸ See also **non-defining relative clause**.

Language glossary

determiner

A determiner is a word that goes at the beginning of a noun group. Determiners include

- the articles *the* and *a*/*an*
- possessives like *my* and *his*, as in *his* friend
- demonstratives like *that* and *these*, as in *these* people
- amounts like *all* and *a few*, as in *a few* mistakes

-ed form

The -*ed* form of the verb, like *arrived*, *played*, *broken*, *seen* and *eaten*, is the form that is used in perfect tenses after *have* or *had*, as in *I've broken it*, and in passive verb chains, as in *Everything was eaten*. (This is also called the past participle.)

ellipsis

Ellipsis is the omission of words when you link groups or clauses together, as in *some intriguing questions and some intriguing answers* → *some intriguing questions and answers*.

finite clause

A finite clause is a clause containing a verb that tells you who or what is doing something (the subject), and the time of the action (past, present, or future). *She danced. She's dancing. She's going to dance.*

▶ See also non-finite clause.

form-based family

A form-based family is a group of words that all have the same stem, like *friend*, *friendless*, *friendly*, *unfriendly*, *friendliness*, *friendship*, and *befriend*. You add prefixes and suffixes to the stem to change either meaning or word class.

▶ See also meaning-based family.

future time

Future time refers to events that will happen in the future. Ways of expressing future time include *The train will arrive shortly*. *I'm going to catch the six o'clock train*. (Some people refer to these as future tenses instead.)

Language glossary

imperative

The imperative is the simplest form of the verb, such as *stop*, *go*, *listen* and *look*. Imperative clauses are used to give commands, instructions, and suggestions, especially on packaging and in manuals, recipes, and advertisements. *Take one tablet twice daily. Eat lots of fruit and veg. Don't feed the animals*.

infinitive

The infinitive is the simplest form of the verb, like *lose*, *manage*, *get* and *remember*. You use it in verb chains with auxiliaries like *do*, *does*, *are*, *was* and *have*. *Did you wait? Mistakes were made. They have won* first prize. You also use the infinitive after modals, as in *I can swim*. With *to*, it is used after other verbs, as in *I need to think*.

-*ing* form

The -*ing* form of the verb, like *thinking*, *teaching* and *increasing*, is used 1) in present and past tenses, as in *I was working*, 2) as a noun, as in *Teaching is hard work*, and 3) as an adjective, as in *increasing amounts of homework*. (This is also called the **present participle**.)

irregular sentence

An irregular sentence may begin with a capital letter and end with a full stop, but it is abnormal in some way. For example, it may have no verb, as in *No hard shoulder for 500 yards*.

irregular verb

Irregular verbs are different from regular verbs because they don't have the usual -*ed* form like *remembered* or *arrived*. Instead they are all different: *go/went/gone*, *see/saw/seen*, *eat/ate/eaten* and *buy/bought/bought*.

▶ See also regular verb.

link verb

A link verb is a verb like *be*, *seem*, *appear*, and *become*. A link verb is usually followed by a complement, as in *It's becoming much colder*.

Language glossary

main clause

A main clause is a clause that can stand alone, for example *She's always complaining*. Two or more main clauses can be linked together to form a **compound sentence**.

▶ See also **subordinate clause**.

main verb

A main verb is the part of the **verb chain** that tells you what the action or situation is about; it carries the meaning of the action, thought, situation etc, as in *I've been **thinking***. (This is often called a **lexical verb** instead.)

meaning-based family

A meaning-based family is a group of words that are all related in meaning, but that do not have the same **stem**. Some are **synonyms** or **near-synonyms**, like *complain* and *grumble*. Some are **opposites**, like *fast* and *slow*. Others are related because they are all in the same category; for example *hydrogen*, *oxygen* and *helium* are all chemical elements. Others are related because they are parts of the same thing; for example *wheels*, *gears* and *pedals* are all parts of a bicycle. Some groups of words are related in a more general way – they are all in the same general field; for example *nutrition*, *calorie*, *diet*, *organic*, *eat*, *protein* and *fibre* are all words you need for talking about diet and eating habits.

▶ See also **form-based family**.

modal

The modals are words like *can*, *should*, *will*, *would*, *must* and *have to*, which indicate various attitudes to what you are saying. They are usually followed by an **infinitive**, as in *We **might** move house*. (The term **modal auxiliary** is also used.)

non-defining relative clause

A non-defining relative clause gives you extra information about a person, thing or situation, and can usually be omitted. There is usually a comma before it. *She's visiting her 93-year-old mother, **who still lives alone***.

▶ See also **defining relative clause**.

non-finite clause

A non-finite clause is a subordinate clause that often has no subject. It contains a verb that does not indicate the time of an action (past, present or future), for example *While walking to his car...* The necessary information is contained in the main clause: *he remembered he had to go shopping* (past).

noun

A noun is a word that names or identifies a person, thing, situation or idea. There are three kinds: concrete nouns, abstract nouns and proper nouns. Different nouns can also be classified as count nouns, uncount nouns, and collective nouns, according to their grammatical behaviour.

noun group

A noun group is a noun combined with other words such as determiners, adjectives, other nouns, and prepositional phrases, such as *my opinion*, *good food*, *the party leader* and *a waste of time*. The main noun is the **head** of the noun group. (The term **noun phrase** is sometimes used instead.)

object

The object is the part of the clause that tells you who or what the action of the verb is 'done to', or is affected by the action in some way. It usually comes after the verb. Objects are usually noun groups or pronouns. *The house has **three floors**. I enjoyed **that**.*

▶ See also subject, verb, complement, adverbial.

open class

The open classes are nouns, verbs, adjectives and adverbs. There are many thousands of words in each class, and new ones are coming into the language all the time.

▶ See also closed class.

opposite

An opposite is a word that has the opposite meaning to another word in a form-based or meaning-based family, for example *useful* → *useless*; *good* → *bad*. (This is also called an **antonym**.)

Language glossary

passive verb chain

A passive verb chain occurs in a clause whose subject is the person or thing that is 'done to' by the action of the verb, or that is affected by it in some way. *The kids **have been fed**. The house **will be sold**. The match **was cancelled**.*

past tenses

The past tenses indicate that something happened or existed in the past. *I **bought** a new mobile. They **were playing** in the garden.* (These are often called the **past simple** and **past continuous** respectively.)

perfect tenses

The perfect tenses indicate that something happened recently, or lasted a particular length of time, or happened before something else. *I **have started** a new course. I'**ve been learning** karate for two years. By the time I arrived, everyone **had eaten** the food. They **had been eating** all evening.* (These are often called the **present perfect simple** and **continuous**, and the **past perfect simple** and **continuous**, respectively.)

person

You use the term person to show who is speaking or writing. **First person** refers to the pronoun *I*, **second person** refers to the pronoun *you*, and **third person** refers to the pronouns *he, she, it* and *they* as well as to people or things, as in *He/she/Joe/The team won the game.*

phrasal verb

A phrasal verb (of the type introduced in this book) is a combination of a verb and an adverb to make a two-word verb with a new meaning, such as *set in, find out, catch on* and *grow up*.

phrase

A phrase is any fixed or semi-fixed combination of words that collocate strongly, and that you use as a unit; for example *how the other half lives, keep your hand in*, and *a different kettle of fish*. Phrases are often quite variable, for example you can *clutch at straws* or *grasp at straws*.

prefix

A prefix is a small group of letters that you add to the beginning of a word, to make a new word of the same word class but with a different meaning, for example *appear* → **dis**appear, *security* → **in**security, and *happy* → **un**happy.

▶ See also **suffix**.

preposition

A preposition tells you about <u>place</u>, <u>time</u>, and <u>links between ideas</u>, as in **in** *the garden*, **at** *six o'clock*, **except for** *the weather*. But prepositions have too many meanings to list in a short book. The most common preposition is **of**, as in *a pint* **of** *milk*, *a cry* **of** *pain* etc.

prepositional phrase

A prepositional phrase consists of a **preposition** followed by a **noun group**, as in **in the garden**, **at six o'clock** and **except for the weather**.

present tenses

The present tenses indicate that something happens or is happening in the present. *I* **play** *football*. *The kids* **are playing** *football in the park*. (These are often called the **present simple** and the **present continuous** respectively.)

pronoun

A pronoun is a word that can be used instead of a **noun group**, as in 'the doctor … **she**'. Pronouns include

- **personal pronouns** like *they* and *them*, as in *We beat* **them**.
- **possessive pronouns** like *mine* and *ours*, as in *That cap is* **mine**.
- **reflexive pronouns** like *herself* or *ourselves*, as in *We taught* **ourselves** *chess*.
- **demonstrative pronouns** like *this* and *these*, as in **This** *is not going to work*.
- **question pronouns** like *who*, *what* and *which*, as in **What** *are you doing?*
- **relative pronouns** like *who*, *which* and *that*, as in *the book* **that** *I need*.
- **'amount' pronouns** like *a few* and *enough*, as in *I'm sure there'll be* **enough**.

Language glossary

proper noun

A proper noun names a person, a country, a continent, a geographical feature like a mountain range, or any organization, restaurant, club, company etc, for example *Kylie Minogue*, *Egypt*, *the North Sea* and *Microsoft*.

question tag

A question tag is a shortened clause that you add to the end of a statement to make it into a question, usually because you want your listener to agree with you or confirm your statement. *He's a great player, **isn't he**?*

regular verb

A regular verb is a verb like ***remember**, **arrive*** or ***happen***, which make their different forms by adding -*ing*, -*s* and -*ed*, as in ***remember/remembering/remembers/remembered***.

▸ See also irregular verb.

relative clause

A relative clause is a subordinate clause containing a verb. The clause gives you more information about a noun group. It is usually introduced by a relative pronoun like *who*, *whom*, *that* and *which*, or by *whose* + noun, as in *the boy **who loved cooking***, *the system **that I use***, *the girl **whose hobby is learning guitar***.

▸ See also relative pronoun, defining relative clause, non-defining relative clause.

relative pronoun

The relative pronouns are ***who**, **whom**, **that*** and ***which**. **Whose*** is used in the same way, but it must be followed by a noun. They introduce relative clauses.

report clause

A report clause is a type of subordinate clause. You use it when you are telling someone what you yourself or another person said or thought, as in *She **promised that she wouldn't be late***. This reporting is often called **indirect speech**. When you quote someone's exact words, using quote marks, this is often called

direct speech. *'We're building a new climbing frame for the kids,'* she explained.

sentence

A sentence is any stretch of words that begins with a capital letter and ends in a full stop. The main types of sentence are simple sentences, compound sentences and complex sentences. A fourth type is the irregular sentence.

sentence linker

A sentence linker is a general term for the words and phrases that you can use to link sentences together. For example, connectives like *therefore* are a type of sentence linker, and so are **sequencing** words like *firstly*, *secondly* and *finally*.

simple sentence

A simple sentence consists only of a main clause, for example *I forgot to lock the back door last night*.

▶ See also compound sentence, complex sentence.

subject

The subject is the part of the clause that tells you who or what is the 'doer' of the action of the verb, or is responsible for it in some way. The subject usually comes before the verb, and is usually a noun group or a pronoun. *The house* has three floors. *He* enjoyed the match.

subordinate clause

A subordinate clause is a clause that cannot stand alone, for example *because she has too much work*. You need a main clause to complete the meaning, for example *She's always complaining*. The three major types of subordinate clause described in this book are adverbial clause, relative clause and report clause.

subordinating conjunction

A subordinating conjunction introduces an adverbial clause. There are subordinating conjunctions of **time**, like *when* and *after*; **place**, like *where* and *wherever*; **condition**, like *if* and *unless*; **reason**, like *because* and *as*; **purpose**, like *in order to*; **result**, like *so that*; and **contrast**, like *although* and *whereas*.

▸ See also **co-ordinating conjunction**.

suffix

A suffix is a small group of letters that you add to the end of a word to make a new word. The new word is often of a different word class, for example *organize* → *organiz**ation***, *possible* → *possibi**lity***, *accident* → *accident**al***, and *normal* → *normal**ly***.

▸ See also **prefix**.

superlative adjective/adverb

The superlative form of an adjective or adverb is the form you use to say that something has more of a quality than anything else of the same kind. *She was **the smartest** kid in the class. That was **the best** day of my life. It is young men who drive **the most dangerously**.*

▸ See also **comparative adjective/adverb**.

synonym

A synonym is a word that has roughly the same meaning as another word in a **meaning-based family**, for example ***gloom*** and ***despondency***; ***lovely*** and ***gorgeous***. Synonyms are not often used in exactly the same contexts, so it is better to think of these words as **near-synonyms** rather than true synonyms.

tense

▸ See **present tenses**, **past tenses**, **perfect tenses**, **future time**.

uncount noun

An uncount noun is a noun that has only one form. Uncount nouns usually refer to **abstract** things like ***advice***, ***luck***, ***poverty*** and ***progress***, or else to substances like ***blood***, ***sugar***, ***smoke*** and ***electricity***. (The term **uncountable noun** is often used instead.)

▸ See also **count noun**.

verb

Verbs are used to describe actions, thoughts, feelings and situations, for example *buy*, *sneeze*, *regret*, *love*, *exist*. The verb is part of the clause, and a typical clause might consist of a subject, a verb and an object, as in *I **bought** a new jacket* (SVO).

▶ See also subject, object, complement, adverbial.

verb chain

A verb chain consists of a main verb and one or more auxiliaries or modals. *Maya **is working**. My bicycle **is being repaired**. I **couldn't sleep** last night.*

vowel

The vowels are the letters *a*, *e*, *i*, *o*, and *u*. The letter u often sounds like a consonant, as in *a university*.

▶ See also consonant.

wh-question

A *wh*-question is a question that requires information. It often begins with a **question word** like *who* or *what*. ***Who was that on the phone?***

▶ See also yes/no question.

word families

Word families are groups of words that are related in some way.

▶ See form-based families, meaning-based families.

yes/no question

A yes/no question is a question that requires only a 'yes' or 'no' answer. It usually begins with an auxiliary or modal, as in ***Have you finished your meal?*** *Yes I have.* ***Can we leave then?*** or with the main verb *be*, as in ***Are you a footballer?***

▶ See also *wh*-question.

Answers to activities

Part 1

Activity 1 Before you start (page 3)

Words that can be exchanged:

imagined, thought (verbs)

imaginative, thoughtful (adjectives)

imagination, thoughtfulness (nouns)

Activity 2 Concrete and abstract nouns (page 7)

1 concrete: **lamp, flame, onion, layer, pod, walls, crystal, seas;** abstract: **space, view**

2 all abstract

3 concrete: **panther, shape(?), eyes**; abstract: **growl(?), sight, yards, intelligence**

Activity 3 Proper nouns (page 8)

1 the Labour → **c** Party

2 the Taj → **d** Mahal

3 South → **e** Africa

4 Mount → **b** Kilimanjaro

5 the European → **a** Parliament

Activity 4 Irregular plural nouns (page 8)

leaf → leaves

foot → feet

mouse → mice

woman → women

crisis ➜ crises

valley ➜ valleys

half ➜ halves

fish ➜ fish, fishes

sheep ➜ sheep

Activity 5 Identifying nouns (page 9)

1 They haven't been given adequate **training**. (noun)

2 I hated the name from the very **beginning**. (noun)

3 They were all **beginning** school at the same time. (verb)

4 Alpine resorts are **suffering** from a lack of snow this season. (verb)

5 I'll probably be **training** on Monday again. (verb)

6 Lucy seemed to be blind to their **suffering**. (noun)

Activity 6 Count and uncount nouns (1) (page 11)

1 count: **lungs**; uncount: **air, blood, carbon dioxide, oxygen**

2 count: **job, friends, opportunities, career**; uncount: **money, support, hope**

Activity 7 Count and uncount nouns (2) (page 11)

1 Forgery and fraud are both serious crimes. (count)

2 Petty crime always seems to increase at Christmas. (uncount)

3 DNA evidence proved that he had not committed the crime. (count)

4 Remember the slogan 'Tough on crime and tough on the causes of crime'? (uncount)

5 Mary has never actually been charged with a crime. (count)

Answers: Part 1

Activity 8 Before you start (page 14)

You might have chosen these verbs:

1 I **ran** home and **watched** some more football, **changing** channels whenever they **showed** a commercial.

2 Winston **raised** his eyebrows and **looked** at me in surprise.

3 Andy **asked** me to **give** him your number, but I **refused**.

4 We dashed across the car park, **threw** our cases into the car, and **drove** off.

5 I **sprained** my left ankle while **playing** football.

6 Farmers now **find** it harder and harder to **make** a living.

Activity 9 Verb forms (page 15)

1 He suddenly **remembered** a boy at school who'd looked exactly the same as Matt.

2 The police want her to revisit the scene in the hope that she may **remember** a vital clue.

3 **Remember**, this is a long trip and you'll need to be prepared for the jetlag.

4 I wanted to **remember** every moment of that day for ever.

5 You could at least have **remembered** to water the plants!

There are no other possibilities.

Activity 10 Irregular verbs (page 15)

Here are ten irregular verbs. You may have thought of others:

begin, began, begun

catch, caught, caught

cut, cut, cut

give, gave, given

hear, heard, heard

make, made, made

put, put, put

say, said, said

Answers: Part 1

take, took, taken

write, wrote, written

Activity 11 Before you start (page 16)

1 Where **did/do** you **buy** that?

2 The British **have eaten** eels for centuries.

3 When she reached them, she **was smiling** broadly.

4 I thought you **had left** ages ago!

5 Guide dogs **are allowed** but the Peke stays outside.

Activity 12 Auxiliaries – present tense (page 17)

1 At the moment I **don't** see what any of this means.

2 Why **don't** you wear your red dress with the silver belt?

3 Even if they are wrong, what difference **does** it make?

4 I think Maria's family **doesn't/don't** like the English weather at all.

5 '**Do** spiders ever get tired of climbing walls?' she wondered.

'Family' is a collective noun.

Activity 13 Auxiliaries – present and past tense (page 18)

1 I like Leroy because he **doesn't disrespect** my beliefs.

2 **Did** she **give** you any clue as to her real identity?

3 What on earth **do/did** they **talk** about all day?

4 Call me if his condition worsens, but I **don't think** it will.

5 I **don't eat** much junk food, but I **do like** an occasional bag of crisps.

Activity 14 Auxiliaries – mixed tenses (1) (page 21)

1 More politicians → **c** are hinting at tax increases.

2 According to health experts, I → **e** was simply eating too much.

3 My neighbour's daughter → **a** has been babysitting the kids.

4 Not one person → **b** has come up with a solution.

5 Paul and Gek Ling → **d** have found their ideal home.

Activity 15 Auxiliaries – mixed tenses (2) (page 21)

1 You just **don't** know what to believe these days.

2 Mohamed **had/has** picked up the phone from the desk, and **was/is** playing with it.

3 This is the worst food I **have** ever tasted.

4 Neither of his books **is** selling very well at the moment.

5 Usually they went for a brisk walk after they **had** eaten.

6 In the 1990s my parents **were** living in Gloucester.

Activity 16 Future time (page 22)

1 I'm excited about the win, but it **won't** change my life.

2 Julie and Wojtek **will be/are** moving to their new house next week.

3 I **will** pay you four pounds an hour if you help with the garden.

4 The electronic version probably **isn't** going to come online anytime soon.

5 Large amounts of snow **are** probably going to fall over the weekend.

In negative sentences, 'probably' comes before the auxiliary. In positive sentences, it comes after the auxiliary.

Activity 17 Time frames (page 24)

1 past: **stopped, called, checked, dialled;** perfect: **had given**

2 past: **rang, buzzed, went, worked;** present: **talk, have**

Activity 18 Modals (page 25)

1 You **can't/shouldn't** take anything for granted in this life.

2 Here are some ideas that you **might/may** like to try out.

3 Dave missed the exit so we **had to** go round the roundabout again.

4 Is there anything else that I **ought to/should** know about?

5 It says on the box that if the seal is broken, you **mustn't/shouldn't** eat them.

Activity 19 The passive – mixed tenses (page 27)

1 Their whole crop **was** destroyed by elephants last year.

2 All your files **should be** backed up regularly.

3 The cliffs **were** formed when the sea level was higher.

4 The country **has been/was** ruled by dictators for decades.

5 We **are/were** not allowed to bring food into the classroom.

6 A lot **can be** achieved if we put our minds to it.

Activity 20 Why choose the passive? (page 28)

1 The sentence is about bread and how it was made, rather than who made it.

2 The verb 'is air-conditioned' is passive because you are not interested in who air-conditioned the places. The verb 'is freeze-dried' is passive because the topic is 'the sweat'.

Activity 21 Why choose the active? (page 28)

The writer uses the active because the subjects of the verbs (the 'doers') are important here. 'Grow' and 'say' have no objects in these sentences, so they cannot be passive. 'Pick' has no subject, as it is imperative.

Activity 22 Verb + *to*-infinitive (page 29)

1 The prime minister refused ➔ **d** to comment further.

2 She managed ➔ **e** to get a job as a gardener.

3 He remembered ➔ **a** to get his parents' permission.

4 I cannot begin ➔ **f** to understand any of this.

5 I promise ➔ **b** to tell the truth.

6 I'm afraid she's starting ➔ **c** to lose consciousness.

Activity 23 Imperatives (page 30)

1 Vote ➔ **e** Lib Dem.

2 Watch ➔ **d** this space.

3 Don't feed ➔ **a** the animals.

4 Drink → **c** more water.

5 Do not spray → **b** this substance in an enclosed area.

Activity 24 Two types of adjective (page 32)

1 The **ancient** Egyptians wore bracelets with **magical** charms dangling from them.

2 She said a bit about her **exciting new** band, then strapped on an **electric** guitar.

3 During this time, my main symptom was **complete** and **utter** exhaustion.

4 Tanya is very **secretive**, and doesn't like anyone to interfere in her **private** life.

Activity 25 Adjective order (page 33)

1 Bathed in **sickly green fluorescent** light, they sat staring at the TV.

2 Today she wore **cool pale blue Indian** cotton.

3 Meena went out and bought a **silly purple chiffon** bubble dress.

Activity 26 Comparative adjectives (1) (page 35)

1 Diesel engines are thirty percent more fuel-efficient than petrol engines.

2 The animals were moved from the zoo to higher ground.

3 He rarely cooked anything more adventurous than spaghetti bolognese.

4 Barbecues are now more popular than ever./Barbecues are more popular than ever now.

5 Since 2000, fashion has become more and more accessible to people.

6 The new show is going to be bigger and better than the last.

Activity 27 Comparative adjectives (2) (page 36)

Over the past two million years, human skulls have gradually got a **flatter** face, **smaller** teeth, and a **less prominent** jaw. The top of the skull has become **rounder** and **larger**, to house the **bigger** brain.

Larger and **bigger** can be used interchangeably.

Answers: Part 1

Activity 28 Emphasizing a comparison (page 36)

1 far, much, a lot, infinitely, a good deal, a great deal, considerably, vastly

2 slightly, a little, marginally, a bit

1 The mass of the Sun is **much/considerably** larger than that of the Earth.

2 Her share of the vote was **slightly** higher than her rival's – 30.1 per cent compared with 29.8.

3 Even the store's luxury breakfast was only £3.25 – **considerably/far/a lot/much** cheaper than Tinto's at £5.95.

4 Victoria has suffered its second driest decade on record, with the drought of 1935–45 only **marginally/slightly** worse.

Activity 29 Superlative adjectives (page 38)

1 Each day we will present the best World Cup selections in our blog.

2 According to a new survey, New York City is the most courteous place on the planet.

3 Childhood is the most vital part of human development.

4 The match is the biggest game in Australian history.

5 I'm afraid she's not the most responsible mother in the world.

Activity 30 Comparatives and superlatives (page 38)

1 He had walked a much **longer** distance than he had intended.

2 The café was very gloomy. I could see why the only customer had chosen to sit in **the furthest/the farthest** corner.

3 They were discussing who was **the most likely/the likeliest** choice from the twelve candidates.

4 She was nice enough to begin with, but became even **more helpful** when I slipped her a twenty.

5 I ate at the Fat Pheasant – not **the greatest** food in the world, or even in Slough.

6 Australia are **more vulnerable** in one-day cricket than in Test Matches.

Activity 31 Adjectives for detail and precision (page 40)

The **bear-like** creature let out a **loud** roar. I stumbled, and fell at the feet of a **small elderly** man, who stared at the creature. I had a **fleeting** impression of his features. He had a **stubby white** beard around his chin, **bushy** white eyebrows, and **corrective** glasses.

Activity 32 Adverbs and adjectives (page 42)

1 He stamped his feet in **helpless** frustration.

2 Good for you – you dealt with the whole problem very **well**.

3 'Ron,' I said **helplessly**. 'Save me. Do something.'

4 And Mrs Wilson here is rather **good** at making pastry.

5 Can too many vitamins be **dangerous**?

6 My team-mates have been **brilliant** and a lot of fans are proud of what I've achieved.

7 Premiership clubs are flirting **dangerously** with bankruptcy.

8 The pressure is on but it's all turned out **brilliantly** for the team.

Activity 33 Time and place adverbs (page 44)

1 'Which direction is the coast?' → **f** 'Eastwards, I think.'

2 'Do you go to the gym?' → **e** 'Sometimes. Not enough.'

3 'Where would you like to sit?' → **d** 'Outdoors, preferably.'

4 'Would you like a shower?' → **a** 'Later, perhaps.'

5 'When will he be released?' → **b** 'I don't know. Maybe never.'

6 'Are you working these days?' → **c** 'Temporarily, yes.'

Activity 34 Degree adverbs (page 46)

1 remarkably → **d** similar

2 utterly → **c** useless

3 somewhat → **b** surprising

4 fully → **e** fit

5 terribly → **a** sorry

Answers: Part 1

Activity 35 Phrasal verbs (page 47)

1 Steam and ashes filled the room as the stew **boiled** over into the fire, putting it out.

2 If they borrow something and give it back damaged, they have to pay for the damage caused.

3 The vaccine's effectiveness wears off over time.

4 She wrote something down, but then immediately crossed it out.

5 I'm afraid you've left out the most important point.

Activity 36 Another very common adverb (page 48)

1 Luckily, he had yet to see the giant spider who had built this atrocious trap.

2 The roof was sagging but hadn't yet collapsed inwards.

3 I raised my eyes to heaven yet again.

4 We need to build two big bonfires – or better yet, fireworks displays.

Activity 37 Adverbs for detail and precision (page 49)

1 'Listen, I'll get the key!' She repeated the words clearly and distinctly. 'I'll get the key and I'll come back!'

2 He went quietly to his lonely bed in the other room and quickly fell asleep. Presently he stirred uneasily and then sat up, wondering why it was so light.

3 Her bereaved parents spoke tearfully about a daughter who had spent her life caring for physically and mentally disabled people.

The phrasal verbs are **come back** and **sat up**.

Part 2

Activity 1 What pronouns refer back to (page 53)

1 I wondered if I was seeing the same things through <u>my eyes</u> that everyone else was seeing through **theirs**.

2 You are not going over to <u>Reem</u>'s house. **She** can come here instead.

3 <u>Constanza</u> pointed both her index fingers towards **herself** – 'movie star!'

4 <u>Most reports of apparent mystical powers</u> are crude and patently false. I ignore **those**.

5 Every time <u>Sid</u> opened his <u>mouth</u>, **he** put his foot in **it**.

Activity 2 Personal pronouns (page 55)

1 The police have released **him**, saying **they** do not believe **he** is much of a threat.

2 'We know that people will have different reactions,' **she** says. 'And we hope **they** all do the right thing.'

Activity 3 Avoiding sexist pronouns (page 56)

Possible answers are:

1 If a thief steals your card, he or she cannot access your personal account.

2 Everyone has a DNA profile that is unique to them.

Activity 4 Possessive pronouns (page 59)

1 I've always been a great → **b** admirer of hers.

2 Helen is a very good → **e** friend of mine.

3 Coaching Wales remains a burning → **a** ambition of mine.

4 Her private life is no → **c** concern of yours.

5 This album is a particular → **d** favourite of mine.

Activity 5 Pronouns – mixed types (page 61)

1 Megan made herself comfortable in the armchair.

Answers: Part 2

2 Their culture is quite different from ours.

3 Mr Twit caught the birds and Mrs Twit cooked them.

4 I looked at the ice-cream and decided to eat some.

5 Janny was wearing an old pair of Robert's khaki shorts. These looked enormous on her.

Activity 6 Reference chains (page 62)

Jack: It's tearing **me** apart to think we're just going to leave your parents but **I** can't see any alternative. Do **you** think they'd understand, Mel?

Mel: **They** would want **us** to do whatever's best for us, Jack. They would want **us** to escape and make a new life for **ourselves**.

Activity 7 Amounts (1) (page 66)

1 Every chemical element is composed of atoms, and at **the** nucleus, at the heart of **every** atom, is the proton, without which **no** matter could exist. Protons are the key to **all** creation.

2 I seemed to hear **a** low whistle, and **a few** moments later a clanging sound.

3 There can be **little** doubt that this tortoise is **an** aboriginal inhabitant of **the** Galapagos Islands.

Activity 8 Amounts (2) (page 66)

The pair of sentences in **1** mean different things.

Activity 9 Prepositions of place (page 68)

1 There were hundreds of people walking **away from** the main square.

2 She piled her books **on top of** her desk.

3 They jumped **into** the train just as it began to move.

4 I found him sitting on a bench **in front of** the restaurant.

5 He has just come back **from** our camp in the valley.

Activity 10 Linking prepositions (page 69)

1 West London missed Cole's wonder goal **thanks to** a blackout.

2 There was nothing in the fridge **apart from** a bottle of champagne.

3 She had to wear blue hair extensions **as well as** a lot of jewellery.

4 **According to** the BBC, a falling tree may have caused the accident.

5 **As for** lunch, most days I brought my own food.

Activity 11 Discussion (page 71)

Some other very common words in English include **the**, **of**, **to**, **a**, **in**, **is**, **it**, **you**, **that**.

Activity 12 Co-ordinating conjunctions (page 72)

1 I'm practising four **or** five hours every day.

2 He tried to contact his former colleagues, **but** they wouldn't talk to him.

3 She came home from the Olympics with two gold medals **and** a bronze.

4 Our high attic room was small **but** adequate.

5 She's getting little **or** no exercise.

6 I left home **and** went to live in New York.

Activity 13 Before you start (page 73)

1 **Although** each face was different, they were all in some way familiar to me.

2 I understood my grandfather's feelings **when** he talked of his life in Africa.

3 **While** Bert was cleaning out the dining room, he had discovered a pile of old yellowing maps.

4 He sought out Joanna **because** he expected her to protect him.

5 **If** you miss another rehearsal, we will find someone else for the part.

Activity 14 Subordinating conjunctions (page 76)

1 He checked the papers through again **in case** he'd missed something.

2 **If** she had stuck to the plan, she'd have been safely at the snake pit by now.

3 Ming wanted to walk home, **even though** he knew it would take over an hour.

4 **As soon as** everyone was ready, Bret coughed and began to speak.

5 A brilliant blue digital display lights up **whenever** a call is made or received.

Part 3

Activity 1 Before you start (page 80)

1 It is wanting luxuries you can't afford that makes you **un**happy and **dis**contented.

2 The winners of the competition then take part in nation**al** and **inter**national events.

3 At his trial the captain claimed that the war was **il**legal and **im**moral.

4 The perform**ance** ended in chaos, much to the amuse**ment** of the crowd.

Activity 2 Prefixes (1) (page 83)

1 **anti**-clockwise: against

2 **mega**star: very big

3 **over**cooked: too much; **pre**prepared: beforehand; **re**heated: again

4 **trans**atlantic: across

5 **mal**nutrition: wrong, bad

Other words you could have chosen are **antibiotic**, **megastore**, **overwork**, **prepacked**, **rewrite**, **transplant**, **malfunction**.

Activity 3 Prefixes (2) (page 84)

1 The surgeons had to join blood vessels of only two **millimetres** in diameter.

2 Signs are written in Chinese and English, and the staff are all **bilingual**.

3 The difference between a **millipede** and a **centipede** is the number of legs each has per segment.

4 This walrus was a huge animal, with tusks about 60 **centimetres** long.

5 London's first **multi-storey** car park was built in 1937.

Activity 4 Prefixes – general knowledge (page 85)

1 A megabyte is 1,000 times bigger than a kilobyte (it is roughly one million bytes). A gigabyte is 100,000 times bigger than a kilobyte (it is roughly one thousand million bytes).

2 Its precise meaning is 'one thousand millionth' (a 'billionth'). A nanosecond is one thousand millionth of a second. A nanometre is one thousand millionth of a metre. Nanoparticles are small enough to be measured in nanometres, and nanotechnology deals with matter measured in nanometres.

Activity 5 Noun suffixes (page 86)

1 education, conclusion

2 appearance, insurance

3 argument, achievement

4 preference, interference

5 farmer, painter

Activity 6 Adjective and adverb suffixes (page 87)

1 preferable, noticeable

2 idiotic, photographic

3 logical, musical

4 endless, harmless

exactly, happily

Activity 7 More suffixes (page 87)

1 hand**ful**: suffix means 'the amount held by'; the word is a noun.

2 hand**ful**: suffix means 'the amount held by'; the word is a noun.

3 remark**able**: suffix means 'worthy of' (ie worthy of remarking on); the word is an adjective; pain**ful**: suffix means 'characterized by' or 'having'; the word is an adjective; honest**y**: suffix means 'the quality or state of being'; the word is a noun.

4 employ**ee**: suffix means 'the person affected by an action'; the word is a noun.

5 child**hood**: suffix means 'the state of being'; the word is a noun.

6 nightmar**ish**: suffix means 'similar to'; the word is an adjective; slow**ly**: suffix means 'in a … way'; the word is an adverb.

7 small**ish**: suffix means 'somewhat, quite'; the word is an adjective.

8 flame**proof**, oven**proof**: suffix means 'able to withstand'; the words are adjectives.

9 pesti**cide**s: suffix means 'killing'; the word is a noun.

Handful does not mean the same in **1** and **2**. In **1**, it means 'a few', in **2**, it means 'the amount you can hold in your hand'.

The suffix **-ish** does not mean the same in **6** and **7**. In **6**, it means 'similar to', and in **7**, it means 'somewhat'.

Some words with the same suffixes are: **cupful, mouthful, objectionable, graceful, jealousy, interviewee, adulthood, childish, happily, oldish, waterproof, insecticide**.

Activity 8 The suffix '-style' (page 88)

1 The houses come complete with American-style hot tubs and saunas.

2 Firefighters in Surrey battled hundreds of Australian-style bush fires.

3 Meals are served family-style, and everyone gets to know each other.

4 A Mediterranean-style diet is rich in olive oil, whole grains, and vegetables.

5 A 'fat-free' French-style salad dressing may have eight per cent sugar, plus stabilizers and colourings.

Activity 10 'affect' or 'effect'? (page 91)

1 Changes in sea temperature **affect** penguins and seals in the Antarctic.

2 The biggest **effect** of the floods is people's shattered lives.

3 The mercury in fish has harmful **effects** on living organisms.

4 New technologies **affect** almost everyone, whatever their age.

5 We need to know more about the causes and **effects** of global warming.

6 All train services in the area **are affected** by the floods.

Activity 11 Verb or noun? (page 91)

1 noun

2 verb

3 verb

4 noun

5 noun

Activity 13 Before you start (page 94)

1 opposites

2 different words meaning 'dirty' (near-synonyms)

3 different animals (same category)

4 a sentence can be part of a paragraph, a paragraph part of a chapter, a chapter part of a section, a section part of a book

5 words related to the idea of 'television' (fields)

Activity 14 Near-synonyms (page 95)

1 I lay on the mattress with only a **thin** blanket over me.

2 Choose **lean** cuts of meat and trim off any fat.

3 She poured wine into tall, **slender** glasses.

4 **Scrawny** chickens and ducks scrabbled in the dust for scraps.

5 The jacket could be worn with a **slim** black skirt.

6 In the no-mercy world of fashion, **skinny** jeans are back.

Answers: Part 3

Activity 15 Categories – general knowledge (page 97)

Here are some of the words you may have thought of. There are many others:

1 aluminium, helium, silver

2 alligator, chameleon, tortoise

3 rhombus, sphere, trapezium

Activity 16 Parts – general knowledge (page 97)

Here are some of the words you may have thought of. There are many others:

1 chassis, clutch, mirror

2 fruit, leaf, root

3 keyboard, motherboard, mouse

Activity 17 Word fields (page 98)

Here are some of the words you may have thought of. There are many others: **access**, **broadband**, **cookie**, **download**, **firewall**, **hypertext**, **link**

Activity 18 Compound nouns (page 99)

1 The full glare of the **spotlight** again falls on Nicole Kidman.

2 The team developed specialized **software** for analysing genetic data.

3 Australia's vast size makes it difficult to connect every home to a high-speed **network**.

4 Everything inside the computer is connected to a circuit board called the **motherboard**.

5 The Herald has produced a glossy **wallchart** of Scottish birds.

6 Make sure you use a **broadband** connection, as dial-up takes longer.

Activity 19 Compound nouns with 'sun' (page 100)

1 The cat was lying on the doorstep in a patch of **sunlight**/ **sunshine**.

2 Are you expecting us to get through this jungle by **sunset/ sundown?**

3 She wore a chiffon top, silver shoes and wraparound **sunglasses.**

4 If you go to the beach, wear **sunscreen/sunblock**, lots of it.

5 We watched the warm, pink **sunrise/sunset** reflected in the skyscraper windows.

6 **Sunspots** are planet-sized magnets created by the sun's inner magnetic dynamo.

Here are some compounds you may have thought of. There are many others: **sunbathe**, **sundial**, **sunlamp**, **sunroof**, **suntan**, **suntrap**

Activity 20 Compounds with 'free' (page 103)

1 They keep more than 400 **free-range** hens up there in the hills.

2 It will then dive 2400m, the **freefall** allowing passengers to experience zero gravity for around 25 seconds.

3 She won the 100m **freestyle** and came third in the butterfly.

4 Chelsea were awarded a **free kick** in the 18th minute.

5 **Freeware** is software that you can use without paying anything.

Activity 21 Vocabulary knowledge (page 103)

1 Celeste taught him **sign language** and later **lip-reading**.

2 If you go back to the **home page**, you'll find links to all our online services.

3 He needs to show that he can do more than provide a neat **soundbite** for TV.

4 The hot weather meant increased pollution in **city centres**.

5 I thought it was a joke, so I was waiting for the **punchline**.

You may have used other forms of these words, for example **homepage**.

Activity 22 Newer compounds nouns (page 104)

1 A **plasma screen** in one corner was showing a football match.

2 **Climate change** will inevitably increase the risk of flooding.

Answers: Part 3

3 I was a couch potato before I joined the cricket team.

4 Carbon and methane are both greenhouse gases.

Activity 23 Collocation (page 106)

1 So he had to make a **choice** in the end.

2 They have not yet given us a **reason** for the delay.

3 He's made some very rude **comments** about different people.

4 We're going to take/have a **break** now – all of you be back in 15 minutes!

5 I told George that I can't see the **point** of arguing about it.

6 Are they seriously trying to find/reach a peaceful **solution** to the dispute?

7 His plan to hold the **meeting** on Monday fell through.

8 Take/have a **look** at this map.

9 Six thousand viewers complained that the programme set a bad **example** to children.

10 They have found/discovered no **link** between him and any terrorist organization.

Activity 24 Well-known phrases (1) (page 107)

1 I would be happy **beyond my** wildest **dreams** if I could buy a small house for my family.

2 The best doctors, the best nurses, want to work in a hospital that's **on the** cutting **edge** of medical research.

3 Calm down! Losing your mobile is not **a matter of** life and death!

Activity 25 Well-known phrases (2) (page 108)

1 eye

2 shot

3 time

Part 4

Activity 1 Noun groups (page 112)

The Owl (determiner +noun) and the Pussy-Cat (determiner + noun) went to sea
In a beautiful pea-green boat (determiner + adjective + adjective noun),
They took some honey (determiner + noun) and plenty of money (determiner + noun),
Wrapped up in a five-pound note (determiner + adjective + noun).
The Owl (determiner + noun) looked up to the stars above (determiner + noun + adjective),
And sang to a small guitar (determiner + adjective + noun)…

How doth the little crocodile (determiner + adjective + noun)
Improve his shining tail (determiner + adjective + noun);
And pour the waters of the Nile (determiner + noun + prepositional phrase)
On every golden scale (determiner + adjective + noun)!
How cheerfully he seems to grin,
How neatly spreads his claws (determiner + noun),
And welcomes little fishes (adjective + noun) in,
With gently smiling jaws (adverb + adjective + noun)!

Activity 2 Expanding noun groups (page 113)

1 She assured him that he would play **a very active role in the debate.**

2 The support of family and friends at this time is **a great comfort to us.**

3 **The alleged charges against him** were dropped and he was free.

4 The unnecessary use of sprinklers is **a shocking waste of water.**

5 His mother gave me **some beautiful blue glasses** as a present.

Activity 3 Linking noun groups – definitions (page 113)

1 a giant fungus, ➔ **e** the world's largest known organism

2 the blue whale, ➔ **c** the world's largest animal

3 the European hedgehog, ➔ **d** the world's sleepiest mammal

Answers: Part 4

    4 Californian redwoods, → **a** the world's tallest trees

    5 the African elephant, → **b** the world's largest land animal

Activity 4 Linking noun groups – omitting words (page 114)

1 The support vehicle was carrying our new sleeping bags, **our new** tents and **our new** climbing gear.

2 Rich visitors are shopping aggressively for luxury bags, **luxury** watches and **luxury** designer clothes.

Activity 5 Adjective groups with adverbs (page 116)

1 The way football is played in Italy and England is **completely different**.

2 I must say I found her behaviour **slightly odd**.

3 I'll be **perfectly happy** if we get as far as the third round.

4 In spite of the pain, he was feeling **remarkably calm**.

5 Juggling with six balls at the same time is **rather difficult**.

6 My mother had a coat like that – it was **virtually identical**.

Activity 6 Adjective + preposition (page 117)

1 Most local people are **dependent on agriculture** for survival.

2 If you are **allergic to dairy products**, you won't be able to eat yoghurt.

3 As long as the children are **honest with me**, that's all I care about.

4 Some parents are not **good at discussing sex education**.

5 She tries to keep her work **separate from her family life**.

Activity 7 Verb + *to*-infinitive or *-ing*? (page 119)

1 He **suggested exploring** some out-of-the-way places in California.

2 Firefighters **have managed to control** a blaze in south London.

3 We **are hoping to hear** his side of the story soon.

4 I **couldn't imagine spending** the night in a haunted house.

5 We **couldn't afford to feed** ourselves properly back then.

Activity 8 Before you start (page 120)

1 (**1**) The condition is highly infectious (**2**)and passes very easily within families.

2 (**1**) They tested the virus (**2**) to see if it was infectious.

3 (**1**) Called nanotube water, (**2**) these molecules contain two hydrogen atoms and one oxygen atom (**3**) but do not turn into ice.

Activity 9 The structure of clauses (page 123)

1 (**S**) The high altitude atmosphere (**V**) contains (**O**) less oxygen.

2 (**V**) Is (**S**) bird flu (**V**) becoming (**C**) more infectious?

3 (**S**) Lack of oxygen (**V**) causes (**O**) severe damage to the brain.

4 (**S**) Doctors (**V**) were monitoring (**O**) his heart rate and respiration.

5 (**S**) Diamonds (**V**) are (**C**) a natural form of pure carbon.

6 (**S**) Bacteria and viruses (**V**) can weaken (**O**) your immune system.

Activity 10 Adverbials (page 124)

1 The flu virus can invade one million nose and throat cells in twelve hours.

2 Brown the dish under the grill for five minutes, then serve immediately.

3 Plants carry out photosynthesis during daylight.

4 In the late 1800s, the French chemist Louis Pasteur realized that disease was carried by microscopic germs.

5 By the 11th century, the Chinese were using movable type for printing.

The other adverbials are **under the grill, by microscopic germs, for printing**.

Activity 11 Question words (page 126)

1 Who ➔ **e** invented the thermometer?

2 Which animals ➔ **d** use camouflage for protection?

3 Where → **h** does gold come from?

4 How → **g** did Roman merchants weigh things?

5 How long ago → **f** was the wheel invented?

6 What → **b** is a deciduous tree?

7 How fast → **a** could a dinosaur run?

8 Why → **c** are some flowers red?

Activity 12 Question tags (page 127)

1 Dreams do come true, **don't they**?

2 I mean, we never quarrelled or anything, **did we**?

3 'Someone will come to rescue us, **won't they**?' she whispered.

4 'You believed me, **didn't you**?' she cried passionately.

5 He hasn't had any problem with his eyes, **has he**?

Activity 13 Subordinate clauses (page 130)

1 <u>Whenever there was an argument</u>, Tom clammed up.

2 We went skateboarding <u>if the weather was fine</u>.

3 I worked hard on my fitness levels <u>so that I'd be ready to play</u>.

4 <u>Though she was brought up in Singapore</u>, she never learned Chinese.

Activity 14 Non-finite clauses (page 131)

1 <u>When using brown or wholemeal flour</u>, you often need a little more water <u>to give you an elastic dough</u>.

2 By 4000 BC, Sumerian merchants were travelling far and wide, <u>trading food, cloth, pots and knives</u>.

3 <u>Invented during World War II</u>, napalm became especially notorious in the Vietnam war.

Activity 15 Time and place clauses (page 132)

1 Whene'er you meet a crocodile, → **b he's ready for his dinner!**

c **We can argue about this** → **2** until the cows come home.

3 As soon as he saw them → **e he yelled and waved wildly.**

4 When the going gets tough, → **d the tough go shopping.**

5 Wherever children go, → **a they are bombarded with junk.**

Activity 16 Conditional clauses (page 133)

1 If pigs could fly, → **b** I'd fly a pig, to foreign countries small and big.

2 If wishes were horses, → **a** beggars would ride.

3 If all the world was paper, and all the sea was ink, and all the trees were bread and cheese, → **d** what would we have to drink?

4 If you should meet a crocodile, → **c** don't take a stick and poke him.

Activity 17 Different adverbial clauses (page 135)

1 I repeated what I had said → **b** in case anyone had misunderstood.

2 We left home early → **h** so as to beat the traffic.

3 Pedestrians are taking increasing risks → **g** in order to cross the road.

4 State schools in Moscow told students to stay at home → **a** as long as the temperature remained below minus 20 degrees in the morning.

5 The calculations took over an hour, → **e** because she was so bad at sums.

6 In days gone by we filled our coal scuttle or collected wood for the fire, → **c** whereas now we just flick on a switch and expect everything to work.

7 She unpacked her banana sandwiches, → **f** even though she'd eaten breakfast only an hour ago.

8 It is in one of these vaults that the Count sleeps during the day → **d** so that the sunlight may not touch him.

Activity 18 Definitions (page 136)

You might have said:

1 A carnivore is an animal **that** eats flesh.

2 A herbivore is an animal **that** eats plants.

3 Carbon dioxide is the gas **that humans breathe out**.

4 An astronomer is a person **who studies the stars and planets**.

5 Your heart is the organ **which pumps blood round the body**.

Activity 19 Defining relative clauses (1) (page 137)

1 Termites build homes that/which **are as elaborate as a modern tower block**.

2 You're just the person who/0 **I wanted to talk to**.

3 The ancient Egyptians used paper that/which **was made from papyrus reed**.

4 He had a daughter whose **hobby was collecting ancient coins**.

5 She drew a picture of the creature which/that/0 **she had seen**.

Activity 20 Defining relative clauses (2) (page 138)

1 People thought the footprints were those of a big cat λthat/which had escaped from the zoo.

2 There were things going on for λwhich I could find no logical explanation.

3 Mrs Twit had a glass eye λthat/which was always looking the other way.

4 Two of Mum's close relations died recently, including the cousin to λwhom she 'd been very close.

5 Anand had no words λthat/which could adequately express his rage.

Activity 21 Non-defining relative clauses (page 139)

1 A third man, whose **address was not given**, also appeared before the court.

2 Most ancient civilizations were polytheistic, which **means that they worshipped more than one god**.

3 She never forgot about her father, to whom **she wrote a letter every month**.

4 Early sea voyages were plagued by scurvy, which **was known as the seaman's curse**.

5 She introduced me to Shirin, **who/whom she described as 'a very warm-hearted person'.**

Activity 22 Report clauses (page 141)

1 He often **complains** that he doesn't get the respect he deserves.

2 The council **promised** that the repairs to the bridge would be completed by November.

3 Then she **informed** me that her daughter was getting married.

4 His family and friends **denied** that he had anything to do with terrorism.

5 The big tobacco companies failed to **warn** consumers that smoking is harmful and addictive.

6 I asked her how she had got into the house and she **replied** that Jemima had given her the keys.

Part 5

Activity 1 Compound sentences (page 145)

1 Mrs Twit may have been ugly and she may have been beastly, **but** → **c** she was not stupid.

2 Mr Twit caught the birds **and** → **d** Mrs Twit cooked them.

3 The kitchen window opened easily, **but** → **f** climbing in turned out to be tricky.

4 Muggle-Wump and his family longed to escape from the cage in Mr Twit's garden **and** → **a** go back to the African jungle where they came from.

5 Her bare feet ached from running on concrete, **but** → **e** she ignored the pain.

6 The shop wasn't large, **but** → **b** Tamaki found quite a few things she could try on.

Activity 2 Linking in compound sentences (page 148)

1 He taught her not to steal or lie, or be spiteful to other people.

2 People were cheering, singing and dancing in the streets.

3 Gibb's staff cook, clean and cater for his family's every need.

4 The women must cook, clean, chop wood and transport heavy loads on their heads.

Activity 3 Complex sentences (page 149)

1 Fools rush in where angels fear to tread.

2 When in Rome do as the Romans do.

3 Where there's a will there's a way.

4 Don't count your chickens until they're hatched.

5 When the cat's away the mice will play.

6 Don't cross you bridges until you come to them.

Activity 4 Different types of sentence (page 149)

(1) .... Things cling to hairs, especially food. (simple) **(2)** Things like gravy go right in among the hairs and stay there. (compound) **(3)** You and I can wipe our smooth faces with a flannel and we quickly look more or less all right again, but the hairy man cannot do that. (compound) **(4)** We can also, if we are careful, eat our meals without spreading food all over our faces. (complex) **(5)** But not so the hairy man. (simple) **(6)** Watch carefully next time you see a hairy man eating his lunch and you will notice that even if he opens his mouth very wide, it is impossible for him to get a spoonful of beef-stew or ice-cream and chocolate sauce into it without leaving some of it on the hairs. (compound and complex) **(7)** Mr Twit didn't even bother to open his mouth wide when he ate. (complex) **(8)** As a result (and because he never washed) there were always hundreds of bits of old breakfasts and lunches and suppers sticking to the hairs around his face.(compound and complex)

Activity 5 Irregular sentences (page 151)

1 description in clothes catalogue

2 newspaper headline

3 advert for travel destination

4 newspaper or magazine headline

5 advert for watch

6 newspaper headline

Activity 6 Connectives (page 154)

1 She wasn't travelling with anybody, **therefore** nobody reported her missing during the cruise.

2 Often he'd go for hours without speaking at all. Maya, **on the other hand**, could not be silent.

3 Isabelle was rather enjoying her new fame, after so many years. **Nevertheless**, she did not allow it to turn her head.

4 The pillows had been ripped apart, and feathers covered my bed, the floor, the table. The sheets were **also** ripped.

5 Many parents have to go to work, which limits the time they can spend with their children. **In addition**, children are involved in school and other activities.

6 Some countries have more efficient medical services than others. **For example**, let's take a look at Cuba.

Activity 7 Showing your opinion or attitude (page 156)

1 **Actually**, now I come to think of it, I did notice this morning that my trousers weren't quite so tight.

2 **Sadly**, global warming is melting the polar bear's world and along with it his chance to feed, reproduce and ultimately survive.

3 **Naturally**, I understand and sympathize. I've been there myself.

4 **Typically**, January and February are the worst months for flooding.

5 **Fortunately**, there is now a vaccine that will prevent girls from getting cervical cancer.

6 **Unfortunately**, Hollywood still glamorizes smoking.

Activity 8 Different sentence linkers (page 157)

1 To insert an arrow into your text, go to the toolbar and select Insert, Symbol. **Next**, scroll down until you find the arrow you want. Press Insert, and **then** close the box.

2 The men sit around the fire and tell hunting stories. **For example**, one tells how he killed a crocodile that was as long as the river is wide. **Naturally** , everyone knows that the stories are greatly exaggerated , but it is entertaining.

Answers: Part 5

3 Selina knew she should have been editing a glossy fashion magazine in Manhattan. **Instead** , she was sitting in a poky little office next to Sammy's barber shop.

4 Ever since then, he had made one mistake after another. **Probably** he had just made another one by missing this golden opportunity.

5 **Oddly enough**, 72 percent of the American public does not know that plastic is made from petroleum products, primarily oil. **Moreover** , 40 per cent of the respondents believe that plastic will biodegrade at some point.

Activity 9 Referring back (page 159)

1 In the past Terry and I had always worked through our problems. This time **we** would just have to **do so** again.

2 'I may seem to be sentimental, Jessie, but basically I'm a practical man . You do understand **that** don't you?' 'Why, of course!' **she** replied, looking surprised.

3 'I think they'll come down through the mountains and attack us.' Masha's voice sounded shaky as she said **this**.

4 'Jetta! Jetta!' called Ginny. The tabby tomcat saw her and ran to **her**. **He** dropped a dead mouse at her feet . All his life Jetta had been bringing his human friends such gifts. But did they appreciate **it**? Never.

Activity 10 Linking sentences logically (page 162)

They were now staring at a sagging greenhouse and an old cucumber frame. Every pane of glass of both **was** (change of tense 1) broken. **However**, (change of linker 1) there was a gorgeous fresh tangy smell in the air. At first Paula **couldn't** (change of tense 2) work out where it was coming from. She sniffed a couple of times, wondering. **Then** (change of linker 2) she **laughed** (change of tense 3) and looked down at their feet. **They** (linker 'in fact' removed) **were** standing (change of tense 4) on an overgrown carpet of mint, the scent of which rose to their nostrils in the cold morning mist. Paula **thought** (change of tense 5) it was sad to see so much neglect.

Activity 11 Varying clause and sentence types (page 163)

You could have rewritten the passage as follows:

When school started again in September, my brother and I took a different route to school on our bicycles. The reason was simple greed, because in the nearby woods there were lots of sweet, juicy blackberries. We ate as many as we could. Often we forgot about the time and we'd arrive late at school, running into the classroom with blackberry stains on our faces, fingers and clothes. However, we didn't get into trouble, as everyone in the class had been doing the same thing.

Index

Index

Index

Index